T0209819

Spiritual Development

With the New England Psychic Medium

Jessenia Nozzolillo

BALBOA
PRESS

A DIVISION OF HAY HOUSE

Copyright © 2019 Jessenia Nozzolillo.

All rights reserved. No part of this book may be used or reproduced by any means, graphic, electronic, or mechanical, including photocopying, recording, taping or by any information storage retrieval system without the written permission of the author except in the case of brief quotations embodied in critical articles and reviews.

Balboa Press books may be ordered through booksellers or by contacting:

Balboa Press
A Division of Hay House
1663 Liberty Drive
Bloomington, IN 47403
www.balboapress.com
1 (877) 407-4847

Because of the dynamic nature of the Internet, any web addresses or links contained in this book may have changed since publication and may no longer be valid. The views expressed in this work are solely those of the author and do not necessarily reflect the views of the publisher, and the publisher hereby disclaims any responsibility for them.

The author of this book does not dispense medical advice or prescribe the use of any technique as a form of treatment for physical, emotional, or medical problems without the advice of a physician, either directly or indirectly. The intent of the author is only to offer information of a general nature to help you in your quest for emotional and spiritual well-being. In the event you use any of the information in this book for yourself, which is your constitutional right, the author and the publisher assume no responsibility for your actions.

Any people depicted in stock imagery provided by Getty Images are models, and such images are being used for illustrative purposes only.
Certain stock imagery © Getty Images.

Print information available on the last page.

ISBN: 978-1-9822-1732-7 (sc)
ISBN: 978-1-9822-1731-0 (e)

Balboa Press rev. date: 12/21/2018

This book is dedicated to my mother, children and husband. Without their help, dedication, support, encouragement and love this book would not be a reality. Thanks for believing in me when I was having a hard time believing in myself. You are why I don't stop pushing for healing and growth.

Contents

Spiritual Development Course

Seeing the Soul

"My goal is to get you to understand yourself, your soul, and your soul family so intricately and intensely that you no longer need to question your existence and purpose here on earth.

My goal is to teach you about all the beautiful traits that make you, You. From soul to skin.

My goal is to change the way you view yourself, thus changing the way you view the world.

My goal is to awaken you to the absolute beauty that surrounds us every day while you learn to un-train your mind to see the negative first.

My goal is that after you understand yourself, your soul, and your energy, you find the courage to trust and believe in yourself first and foremost.

My goal is that once you see how amazing and expansive the soul is, you never limit, judge, criticize or stereotype yourself or another again.

My goal is that when you look in the mirror, you see the amazing, unlimited, intricate, dynamic soul you are - just as source intended.

My goal is to help you see yourself so clearly, with so much love, that you begin to change the world."

-Jessenia Nozzolillo

Note from the author:

Please note this book was created to go with the in-person training session that can be booked anytime via my website, but as you will see, the book also stands alone as a solid informational piece. Part of the class includes 3 Akashic Record Reports. One of which is completed using Andrea Hess's "Soul Realignment" modality, in which I am certified. All Akashic Realm channelers have their own specialty. Hers is soul origination and immense damage to our golden web. Her terms and process are her own and are NOT a part of this book. For more information on her work, please check out her personal page online. My specialty and personally channeled information is all I discuss in this book. The connections, guides, and gifts I use to create Report 2 and 3, are the same connections that provided me the information in this book.

Report 1: Andrea Hess soul realignment, soul origins, blocks and initial incarnation

Report 2: current physical body, and current blocks or obstructing past lives

Report 3: spiritual gifts and blocks to those gifts

Besides "regular" psychic medium readings, I also offer in-person and online past life journeying sessions which focus on removing reoccurring blocks and patterns that have burned through your chakra system. These can manifest as emotional blocks, trauma, pain, physical ailments, fears and phobias - just to mention a few.

For more information check out the website: https://www.neweng landpsychicmedium.com/

"In comfort we avoid challenges. Challenges bring about growth. Growth brings about change. Change brings about soul evolution."

-Jessenia Nozzolillo

Thanks to my panel that helped me prepare this fun Q and A!

Q. What are Soul gifts?

A. Soul gifts are energetic gifts found in the chakras of most soul groups. One of my rare abilities is to access the information regarding your specific energetic gifts as well as what is blocking and inhibiting these gifts. These blocks include past and current life trauma.

Q. What are energetic blocks?

A. An energetic block is the ignored emotional body. The layers of repressed emotions will create solid obstructions. With enough layers, we can experience physical ailments and sickness from these blocks. Obstructions can feel like pains, aches, fears, phobias, sickness, depression, and bruised self-esteem just to name a few. Many times, an energetic block can present itself as a shut-down chakra. Chakras are layered and intricate energy centers of the body. These energy centers store information in a filing system. What you find in the chakra depends on the chakra theme. For example, the root chakra is the place where I find deep physical pain, problems with the home, violence, aggression. Any stories, past life or present, that trigger these categories could block this energy center. Additionally, a gift can present itself as blocked because it's being used inappropriately and working against the person. This is usually because they are unaware of the gift. If you are unaware of a gift that you possess, then you are unaware of how it works and cannot protect yourself against it or use it appropriately. People who experience this issue will sometimes have a hard time in public places like malls, schools, and large events.

Q. Why is this important?

A. Well, when one isn't aware of their gifts or are not using them, then they are using them incorrectly. If they are using them incorrectly this can cause pretty extreme issues! I've seen these intense blocks manifest as physical ailments. I have also seen emotional and energetic issues such as anxiety, depression, sadness, fear of leaving the house, phobias, heightened and irrational emotional sensitivity, even addiction and infertility! These can all come from intense and unresolved past life trauma as well as energetic chakra blocks.

Q. What do the gifts look like in the chakra zones?

A. Well, they can look really different depending on the carrier. Usually what I see is multiple gift aspects and then one major gift. *Usually* the major gift is run by its own **guide**! Guides are assigned to us at soul level to help guide us through our life's decisions and train us in our gifts. Sometimes they are soul family members, other times they are past versions of ourselves. Understanding where your gifts are, what they are, what blocks and unblocks them, and what guides run them is an amazing, timeless, and priceless gift to anyone, especially in getting an upper hand. The stronger our connection to higher-self gets, the quicker we can manifest, heal, and create the change we seek in this physical experience.

Q. Well I'm not a reader...so why is this useful for me?

A. ANY career can benefit from understanding who you are at soul level! If you know your energetic gifts you will know your strengths and how to use them for any career you choose. The gifts are going to be there whether or not you use them. The only difference is that they will inhibit and act against you, possibly causing you many of the issues mentioned above. OR you can begin to work with them, understand them, and use them to your advantage. For example, imagine you are in sales. Your new-found gifts can now allow you to intuitively feel out your client. After discovering and practicing your gifts, you would be better adapted to consciously see/feel what you clients are looking for and what works best for them. It will help you relate better to any job. Healing, life, career, teaching, writing, selling... whatever it may be, I've seen it help so many people! Truly amazing. Learning to use your intuitive abilities and spiritual gifts is also imperative for understanding and connecting to our guides and higher-self. They guide us constantly; whether it be in the area of financial guidance, relationship advice, or life and direction, they do come through. Our connections to our deceased loved ones also get stronger in the process, removing the illusion of separation the human form has created.

When I was younger, I suffered tremendously because of my gifts. I didn't understand why I was so hypersensitive to my environment, others' thoughts and emotions, and surroundings. I didn't have anyone to assist and direct me in my own spiritual evolution. It was difficult. I cried every time someone was hurt. I couldn't stand to be in the city because I felt all the pain, poverty, and struggle. I could not handle public places like schools or malls. I was simply too sensitive and absorbed my environment inappropriately. Seeing beasts of other dimensions, seeing deceased relatives, and knowing things about others I shouldn't was all very overwhelming for me as a child. I didn't know I was gifted or sensitive. I just thought I was broken.

The worst part was that we had a difficult life. As a child, I struggled with poverty, homelessness, sexual/verbal/physical abuse, addicts and dealers. We also moved more than fifteen times before I was ten. Aside from not being able to handle malls, I had a hard time just processing my reality in my daily life. Still, even as a child I remember thinking

"I know someday I will use this information to help others. Someday I will be able to run multiple charities and teach others through my experience." Now I know this was my higher-self giving me hope and reminding me of all the beauty my future would hold, if I could make it that far. I just had to have faith and believe that those were the words of guidance and not the imagination of a desperate child.

In high school, my gifts got so intense that I blocked out most of my high school experience. Sometimes I would get home, "wake up", and realize that I didn't know what happened all day. This made it easy to leave people and move on. I didn't have the capacity to build long-lasting relationships because I simply wasn't there, conscious and aware for the most part.

As a young adult I let my upbringing dictate my future. I had no positive male role models in my life growing up. Not one. I just decided that this was normal. I thought love was just for the movies. I didn't believe that people fell in love, I thought they fell into comfort. I truly believed the world was a dark place full of pain and violence. I refused to watch T.V. and just tried to keep going, not bettering myself but simply existing, simply trying to keep my head above water. Life was not about living, it was about survival. This train of thought understandably put me in dangerous situations. My standards and expectations for people were so low that the worst of the worst were nothing new. The sexual, verbal, and physical abuse and relationships with addicts continued from childhood into my adult years. It wasn't until my early 20's that I began questioning my reality and the patterns and cycles that surrounded me.

I had my oldest daughter while still in high school and my first son right before I began college at 21. My daughter came with me to my high school graduation at just a couple months old, and both my oldest daughter and son were with me when I graduated college. College was when I began to question my reality. I had majored in Psychology with a minor in English and Art. I didn't get far before I noticed change. By the time I received my associate degree, I was already questioning my reality. I was desperately looking for answers and they all fought against what I wanted to believe. For example, sitting in class my psychology professor exclaimed that people are statistically a product of their raising. I didn't want to believe that. I was one of the first in my family to enroll in college and buy a house, all with kids in tow. So, as much as I had been a product of my raising up until this, I felt the desire to continue breaking those chains and barriers my ancestors created. I wanted out and I would not accept that I was created to repeat cycles and patterns and stay stuck. This pushed me. I decided I was human but wouldn't fall victim to the patterns of the human experience. I decided if this reoccurring painful violent pattern was love, then I would rather be alone. I began to plan my new beginning as a single mother of two.

The first day in my own space was heaven to me. I never realized just how much I had been through and experienced until I had a space of my own that was free of abuse, addiction and aggression. My own space was really the beginning of my spiritual journey. I knew I had the ability to be whomever I wanted to be. I was no longer tied down to anyone or any obstacle or any pattern. I released myself from the cycles before me and I decided this was my time to start fresh. This brought me to lesson one. That is, you will never truly *see* the soul while you are physically distracted and in survival mode. It will not happen. If your senses are overwhelmed with survival, then they will not be fully tuned into the spiritual messages and energy that surround you.

After I started my life fresh, I began to hike more and spend more time outside. I cleared my mind of trauma. I left behind the pain. I began the long and tedious process of healing and rebuilding myself. I was recreating my image, building a masterpiece with the rubble of my past. Remolding my life and reconstructing my future. I was busy and comfortable being single for the rest of my life.

Then my husband came along and ruined all my plans. We had known each other a couple of years but I never noticed him. He was just in the space. As I mentioned before, I was always detached and in survival mode. So, I didn't notice that he had been at my house or my parties. He remembered me and respected that I was in a relationship, so he never made any kind of move. After I moved out and moved on, he and my cousin would come by to keep me company and check on me. They would come over, watch T.V. and keep an eye on things around the house. Like a flash of lightning, destiny played out. Soon enough we were dating, married, with kids! Still happy. Still in love.

My husband was the first person, outside of my family, who saw my gifts. The rest of my family has gifts, so to us these issues we were having and things we were seeing were just a natural thing we believed everyone experienced. We never really talked about it. We always knew our family was weird, but we were also raised in very religious households, so we didn't talk about those things. We kept our premonitions, gifts, and abilities to ourselves for the most part. Even after I had vivid dreams of my first two babies, months before I became pregnant, I just chalked it up as a normal thing that people do. My husband has an obsession with the paranormal, mysterious, and haunted. He would drag me to haunted houses. Before this, I had never experienced a haunted house because I saw souls all the time, so naturally I didn't want to go to a place where multiple souls hung out to terrify people. Finding this fun simply didn't occur to me. Our first haunted house experience was an overnight stay at the Lizzie Borden Bed and Breakfast in Fall River, Massachusetts. I could hear, see, feel, and communicate with the souls in the house. It was intense and overwhelming. I couldn't sleep a wink. My husband passed out in his bed and I elbowed him and said something like "Wake up! Don't leave me alone with these souls, they're everywhere! How can you sleep?!" And he said "Nobody sees them but you. To me this is just a poorly decorated room. Goodnight."

And it began. Why was I seeing things? What was I seeing? What was the difference between orbs, shadows, deep apparitions, and lighter ones? Why could some people hear them, and others couldn't? What could all this mean? My thirst for knowledge of the spiritual world began.

I attended many classes with my mother as we tried to figure things out. In every class I attended, I realized I already knew the information. Sometimes, I realized my teachers didn't know the information at all, they simply rehashed what they found on the internet in an innocent attempt at discovering themselves and what they were experiencing. I became skeptical. I thought maybe there is no answer. One day I got completely fed up and thought "I can't find a teacher who knows *all* of what I need. I can't find a gifted soul who shares *all* my abilities. I can't find answers or direction." And a voice came to me and said,

"You can't find it because you are here to create it."

So the birth of my process began.

The process laid out in this book is the exact process I channeled when discovering and developing my own intuitive abilities. I received this information through my connections, from my guides, higher-self, God, gods, goddesses and ascended masters.

I struggled for years to first discover that I had gifts at all. Then I struggled trying to figure out how to use what abilities I had been given. My goal is to assist others in discovering the secrets of their soul, so that they may become familiar with who they are at soul level. Understanding your soul allows you to connect the soul to self in **soul reintegration**. In this process we learn what gifts we have, how to resolve any blockages, and to experience our soul in the fullest possible way in this life through healing and repair.

I am a psychic medium but most importantly I channel the Akashic Realm. The **Akashic Realm** is an energetic database of souls and their lives, progression, themes, stories, missions, soul families, soul groups, gifts, traumas, etc. This information in this book is not tied to any specific religion or belief system. It is my own, granted to me by my guides and connections.

Chapter 1

Soul Origins

This is essentially the over simplified version of how gods and goddesses are born. Let's begin by talking about the creation of souls. **Souls** are birthed by **creator**. Creators are what we would consider **gods/ goddesses/deities**. These creators are birthed by planets and stars. Particles in space slowly accumulating over trillions of years create masses. These masses collect and charge energy, the mass eventually accumulates into a planet or star. These stars and planets continue collecting energy, becoming charged and developing personalities all their own. This complex accumulation of energy eventually births a creator. Creator then becomes the "manager" of that planet or stars energy. In our current scientific scope, we can see and measure the physical matter and process, but we have yet to find the tools to measure the energetic matter. One needs to keep in mind that what we experience here on Earth, through our 5 senses is about 1% or less of all that *is*. 99% of our surroundings are not measurable by our human senses, because the physical experience is rare. Even if we have lived 1,000 lives, it is still a spec in our subconscious experience. Our souls are trillions of years old. These creators, or gods/goddesses/deities, are as unique and expansive as the cosmic material that charged and birth them.

They can be more divine masculine or more divine feminine in energy. Not all creators are "balanced". For example, if the planet is charged with more divine masculine energy and debris, the creator would be more divine masculine. The soul group that follows would also be more divine masculine in makeup. It's important to understand that the terms masculine and feminine are human derived terms created to explain human characteristics of what is male and female. Souls truly don't have male nor female. They don't have genitals. When we speak of the divine masculine, we are simply addressing the traits humans interpret as masculine. I bring this up for a specific reason. When a soul group member of a divine masculine god attempts growth on another planet or soul group, they will attempt to balance their divine masculine and feminine. It does not come easily! They generally stay masculine weather or not they have a female body. This means that no, gayness is not a sin. It is simply a soul discovering and attempting to balance its divine masculine with its divine feminine by choosing lives where they can express both. Because they don't have genitals, or sexes, souls truly have no belief system around sex on the physical world except for that it would be consensual and respectful to another's energy. A sacred energy exchange. All this shame regarding sex, fear of judgment, fear of temptation, homophobia; these are all human created obstructions and limitations.

After their birth, creators begin intentionally evolving the planet or star by manipulating the surrounding energy. They also take over the creation and birthing process of new souls. These new souls they birth are considered a **soul group**. If their planet can sustain life forms, creators would then begin the process of building and sustaining life on their planet. Life forms are not a necessary part of the soul creation and survival process, more like a bonus ability. Not all planets are able to sustain life forms. In this instance the soul group would develop and evolve themselves at soul level with what has been established in their dimension by creator. Creator has the knowledge obtained through the planet or star's accumulation and birthing process. This knowledge includes pre-established energetic codes and programs passed on from dead planets and stars and the cosmic debris they left behind. This works like **cosmic DNA**. This cosmic DNA is something that evolves every time a planet or star is destroyed and restructured into another. On top of the previous jobs listed, creator uses these codes to create a dimension within themselves and life forms if applicable. Life forms are not a part of a dimension. They become a physical world of their own. A **dimension** essentially being an energetic world within a creator for the creator's soul group. Realms are different. A **realm** is a created place outside of a dimension. A realm is created by soul groups, not by creators. The souls birthed in a soul group evolve themselves by experiencing all the fragments in their soul group. This sharing process happens when souls experience themselves in new forms, through interconnectedness. In essence, we evolve at soul level through understanding and working with each other and through our soul level relationships. A sacred energy exchange on soul level. Discovering our weaknesses and strength in others. Absorbing and giving energy in complete balance, or Karma. We give what we take. We take what we need. We give what we can. All in the name of evolution and growth, to help balance ourselves out until we are as well rounded as creator. Once we've experienced our whole soul group, we become a **master soul**. This is incredibly complicated to accomplish. To put this into perspective, humans are about 1/1,000,000 fragment of their higher-self. A large chunk of master-self must stay present on the soul dimension to look over the consecutive lives. They have anywhere form 0-1,000 incarnations on earth if they choose and then must work through their own soul group evolving and understanding them. One could have hundreds or billions in their own soul group. Then one must master creator. If our home dimension was created of 100 strains of cosmic DNA, then we would have 100 X 1,000,000 (or how ever many souls resided in that dimension) souls to meet and master before we could merge to creator. Creator having 100 strands of cosmic DNA is like having the knowledge of 100 dead planets, its inhabitance, soul group and dimension. So yes, it's a lot of work. Its more years than I want to bother counting. We are but a spec…makes dealing with your annoying co worker seem a little miniscule doesn't it?

We can master a dimension and physical planetary incarnations simultaneously or at different times. All creators are interconnected through portals (unless they have been severed for safety) so even if we are at different corners of the cosmos, we still have access to home and each other. You don't need to master your home or soul dimension to move onto a physical incarnation, but some choose to. Some souls take on one challenge at a time, it's a personal preference. Once you master your own dimension, you are granted access to depart freely and become a part of other dimensions. You can temporarily travel before mastery, but not permanently separate yourself from home. It's essentially like being granted a travel visa (temporary travel access for an incarnation) vs being a duel citizen (master soul moving on to master more and establish themselves elsewhere). Even after we become master soul of one soul family, we are driven to master all soul families whose debris, or cosmic DNA, collected to birth our personal creator so that we may reintegrate with our creator. In this way, we always come back home. This process is infinite and gets more and more complicated as time passes. Once we've experienced everything in our creator's cosmic DNA, we are complete. Usually one brings home more information than creator, as you may have spent time in dimensions or planets that are not a part of creator's cosmic DNA, also assisting your creator in the evolutionary process. A team. This can take millions or even trillions of years depending on the cosmic DNA that birthed our creator. But time doesn't exist outside of physical planets and souls are immortal, so it gives us plenty to do! Because creators are planets and dimensions, we do need a creator to survive. So if we leave one creator or home, we move to another that can sustain us. In this way, anyone telling you that we don't do anything when crossing over, simply isn't aware of the complexity of our souls. That's ok! There are millions of people across the world who are not ready to comprehend the depths of our soul essence.

Creator carries its soul group in its energetic body. In this way, creator is its own dimension and home to their soul group. If the planet or star is destroyed, the dimension master soul has created stays with its spiritual inhabitance or soul group. The material of the planet expands outward as the maxed energy implodes to create an opposite reality where the creation process begins on the other side. Sometimes the inhabitance go with the destructed star or planet, unless they have evolved enough to leave the planet. Fragments of the planet or star are then sent off in broken clumps of cosmic DNA, traveling the cosmos looking for another place to land and restart the process. As mentioned previously, part of the creation and structure process is establishing doors and portals to other dimensions and planets. After a planet or stars destruction, we continue using those portals and doors to travel between dimensions. After a planet or star is destroyed, the creator can no longer make new souls, so creator then focuses its energy on evolving its population through experience. Through evolution, mastery and knowledge the soul group gets closer to their goal, **master soul.** One with every soul on your dimension. Eventually as master soul evolves, it would join other dimensions or planets and eventually other master souls and so forth in a never-ending cycle that feeds and fuels space and life. They create us, we maintain them for infinity. The integration of master souls happens more frequently than we think. We will discuss this more in the section regarding ancient souls.

After a planet or star births a creator, creator begins establishing a method, belief system or system of order. The size of the soul group is based off the planet or stars longevity and creator's ability to do its job. Essentially, a thriving soul group is so, because of its creator's ability to collect, structure and manipulate energy with the intention of birthing new souls. This process is fed by ego. **Ego** essentially being a programed survival mechanism to maintaining, expanding and creating soul groups. A drive for expansion and growth. The tool of the gods. You see, ego isn't all bad, it is essentially a survival mechanism. Ego is simply too large for the individual soul to digest and understand. Because ego is a survival tool created for the gods/goddesses/deities, it's easy to see how just a little does us plenty of damage. We are all children of our creator thus we carry ego at soul birth. But because we are not creator, our ego will then misplace itself in other aspects of our lives, feeding false belief systems and separation. The person eventually feeling like they can create or destroy their equals by having more power or knowledge over them. Incorrectly placed ego being the birth of everything that separates us. Every jealous, angry, judgmental expression of separation. The self-destructive belief that they are somehow better or more valuable than their surroundings. In many ways, conquering ego helps us get closer to soul mastery and closer to creator who is the only being who uses ego appropriately. We must master our use of ego to **ascend** or raise our **vibration** and get closer to our creator. Ascension and higher vibrations come when we shed lower level energies associated with ego in the individual soul state. We do this through experiencing and working with each other through our incarnations or soul group. Working for the collective evolution of our soul group, master soul and creator.

Some smaller stars and planets create smaller soul groups and gods, others creating larger ones. This process of accumulating enough energy to birth a creator takes trillions of years. Many of the currently thriving soul groups derived from planets and stars that have been gone too long to note. Meaning a lot of the information connected to their origins was lost in time and translation.

This loss of information created the **Akashic Database.** The Akashic Database is a highly protected realm that now houses all the information we have gathered at soul level so that it may never be lost again. Many times, readers will lump these soul groups into themes and not by creator. This is because not even the Akashic Realm has that information. Someone might say you are of a particular soul group, but essentially, they are lumping you into a known category because your origins are essentially unknown to even the akashic database. For example, we are currently not sure where the Angelic soul group and its God where born. Its star being too old to track. We do know they were born outside of our galaxy, in a galaxy with similar beings and energetic DNA to their soul group. They have since mastered their own galaxy and moved on to ours. Angelic souls now essentially being the accumulated mass of their own galactic conquest, the masters of their galaxy. This mastery isn't violent and aggressive. It is simply the accumulation of knowledge and energy that created their galaxy. With every piece of knowledge they absorb, they expand and change. Their name and image have also been altered with their energetic expansion. They will likely stay the way they are in our human life time, as this expansion and evolution takes billions of years. The Angelic soul group encompasses a large space of existence and expansive knowledge. They are considered a **soul group cluster**. The energy and knowledge of their home galaxy lives on through their energetic body and memory, even if the physical planets and stars do not. **Universal memory** in the collective memory of all the souls, beings and planets born and created in the universe. Universal memory feeds into the **collective multiverse memory**, so yes, limitless, expansive, beyond our comprehension. The issue with universal memory is we must travel to obtain it. Its memory system is not a physical location, place or thing. It is expansive and limitless knowledge, spread all over the universe. In this way, we work for our knowledge. Expansion, exploration, experience and travel equal knowledge.

Now let's talk about "**Hell**", and the great divisional barrier of the "**underworld**". Hell is more like a mirror image of our multiverse. Equal in side but opposite in goals and method. **The other side**. As we lower our vibration we eventually pass through the barrier where everything is opposite and equal. The black matter in the multiverse. The door to the other side. Some beings transfer freely between the barrier, but this is rare. Hermès is one of those beings. The other side is much like ours in creation. Everything must be opposite and equal. Because of this, many of the established energies on the other side of the barrier can't physically live or thrive in our energy or space. Their compositions are just different. It's similar to us trying to touch the depths of the ocean floor. The pressure isn't suitable for our material composition. As is above so is below. Some soul groups thrive in chaos. That is simply who they are and how they were created. As they begin evolving, they eventually transfer through the barrier into the other side where chaos thrives. If a soul is far too destructive to heal, it would then transfer through the barrier. I've only ever seen this once in this life. It wasn't because they cheated on their spouse or did ONE SINGLE bad thing. It was because they murdered, raped and mutilated people for a living, and enjoyed it. But most importantly because they had lived millions of lives doing the same.

The process its self is simply a process of order. As planets collect "dark" cosmic DNA. As they densify, and the creator is established, the creator begins birthing soul groups in their image and then the dimension and group begin the process of working to get closer to their home. When a planet or star implodes, it creates the exact and opposite on the other side. So if there was a thriving planet you may find a destructive planet full of lower level energy and chaos with a soul group and creator to match. We fuel each other. This equal and opposite pull and balance is how the multiverse thrives and recycles energy. As we know here on earth. No energy is ever lost it is simply repurposed. There is a positive and negative in all things. It's important to understand that this applies to all soul groups existing in our multiverse. It is not a religious belief, simply the law of energy and vibration.

In most soul groups who are trying to ascend on this side of the barrier, one must believe and act in inclusivity, oneness, compassion, kindness, empathy and love. This is essential because on this side of the barrier we ascend or raise our vibration through mastering and merging. Our goal is to encompass all knowledge that is, and this means merging. There is no growth in separation on this side. Those individuals who thrive in ego thrive in division and exclusivity. They separate themselves from the collective. They harm their brothers and sisters. They lie and hurt people. They lack and refuse to gain compassion time and time again. The more we hurt our brothers and sisters, the more we separate ourselves from the collective, our energetic vibration gets denser until eventually we tear through the barrier on the side of disorder and chaos. As our planets and stars implode in the multiverse, they tear through this barrier creating the exact equal and opposite on the other side of the barrier. Some planets or stars are created there through the same process as this side and they may work to shift or ascend though the barrier into our side.

Some people attribute this to the commandments and hell. It's easy to see how they were confused. The issue is we only need understanding of the process. This is not a punishment, you don't get thrown in hell for making a bad choice. It takes millions of life times of decisions to descend to the barrier and that is a choice made by the soul and physical incarnations of the soul. We must remove judgment from the process. There is no wrong or right. Some people are drawn to the barrier. Some people love the dark and that is ok. Equal and opposite. We must focus on ourselves and our soul. For every soul that crosses the barrier, one ascends. It's important to understand that one isn't punished for doing "bad" but by choosing separation and lower level energy and emotional density you come closer to the barrier. This is not a one life choice. Or even 46 lives of devotion. It is a million, or sometimes billion-year process of intentionally lowering your own vibrational energy until you pass through the barrier.

The barrier has dimensions, soul groups and planets all its own. It's important to understand "raise" and "lower" are simply directional terms to express "opposite". Raising our vibration shifts are frequency and as we raise our frequency we move further from the barrier. But it's also important to understand that this barrier is more like a mirror image. Side by side not actually up and down. A spectrum of vibration.

Souls are immortal, expansive, energetic bodies with personalities, characteristics, gifts and abilities all their own. Earth has its own creator. Out of all the planet and stars that are created, inhabitable planets are rare. This means that creators without inhabitable planets are drawn to the inhabitable planets so that their soul group may continue to evolve and expand themselves. So even though Earth has its own creator, it has been overwhelmed by multiple creators. Earths creator essentially being the "Earth God" and responsible for "Earths beings" and "Earth dimension". This soul group is a fairly small soul group and its are beings very connected to Earth. The Earth Creator does get upset that so many of its foreign residents, or foreign soul families, are not helping maintain and protect Earth. Seeing Earths destruction is going against the Earth creator's ego program of expansion and growth. The Earthly soul group feel a deep desire to coexist with Earth and keep Earth alive. Many times, the Earth soul group express themselves in their incarnations as environmental activists and humanitarians. Now, this is not to be confused with grounding and programing. All soul groups currently inhabiting Earth need a grounding program so that they may connect to Earth's atmosphere. Some grounding programs need to be more complicated than others depending on the soul group and their cosmic DNA. This drive and connection to Earth is not as extreme as the connection the Earthly beings feel. They require no program. It is simply who they are.

It's easy to see why so many belief systems exist here on Earth given that so many soul families reside here. Remember, creators stay in their dimension parenting their respective soul groups. Creators don't incarnate. They experience, learn and evolve through their soul groups incarnations and travels. They themselves, are too expansive for the human form.

The only way to tie the soul to the extreme density of Earth, was by using Earthly vessels, or bodies. This began as simple life forms. Some of the more complicated **life form codes** where brought in with other soul groups from established inhabitable planets with similar atmospheres to Earth. In Earths early existence, the majority of the soul families inhabiting Earth were of separate small soul groups with different gods and creators, fleeing dead planets, looking for growth etc. Codes are still brought in by healers to this day as a way of reworking and rewriting the physical bodies energy, inventing new things, or creating new structures. Those are all seen as energetic **blueprints** or **codes**. With these established lifeforms, souls could now experience themselves as animals and eventually humans. The side effects of this new experience included denser emotional body and senses we so easily take for granted today; touch, taste, sight, hearing, smell. Emotions are different on Earth and it was not something they were expecting. Earths dense atmosphere also meant dense and heavy negative emotions. Souls found that humans experience anger, jealousy, and pain among other "unfavorable" self-destructive emotions, behaviors, and tendencies. To souls, this became a new project to conquer, resulting in a new stage of evolution for everyone involved. These souls where the original human incarnations. Overtime, other soul groups began building their own Earth programs, so they could also incarnate on Earth.

In this book, I discuss common soul groups that are currently incarnating on Earth and their origins and programmed structure. Humans, mostly, have the same soul structure as the people that surround them. However, there are other soul groups, from different creators, with different energetic construction all around us in less concentrated populations. Regardless of their unique soul structure, only the souls with programs compatible to Earths energy can incarnate here. An **integration program** is the code that allows the soul to connect to the body and environment. Many soul groups are still working on their programs. The information in this book will apply to the majority of the soul groups currently incarnated on Earth, but some soul groups vary in structure thus would not relate to the information provided. They are a rare and small percentage. We can choose to incarnate on other planets, or dimensions, that our soul groups have established integration programs for. Those lives do not always show up in my visions because some life missions are not relevant to our current state of growth. It would be beyond our current perception and understanding. If the information does not serve our current thought process and growth, it's not brought to our attention.

Chapter 2

Meditation And The Chakras

Our **conscious thought** is specifically what we have here on earth—our brain, science, schooling, our earthly limitations. The **subconscious** is our collective soul memories and experience. Your memories and knowledge from every soul and life you've encountered. It is truly limitless compared to our conscious experience. Our brain and human form are unable to process all the information we have experienced through all our lives. It would overwhelm the human form and emotions. Our human mind is highly limited and must process information in linear patterns, so understandably most of our soul information stays in the subconscious mind.

Some information is nearly impossible to comprehend because its language is unlike anything we have experienced in human form. Additionally, some words or visions don't have human translations. For example, many guides' and angels' names are vibrational signatures, not John or Sue. They allow themselves to be called these names because they know their tone and vibrational signature is something us humans cannot vocalize. There are galaxies, planes, dimensions, whole worlds with beings that we simply cannot begin to understand in our human form. Your soul and unconscious understand, it is always connected.

Most people use their subconscious mind irrationally and without direction or understanding. It's really like searching the internet with no purpose. When you are not seeking specific information, you might end up on a website about cat butt jewelry (yes, that's a real thing). In this case, it just distracts us and causes us to wander, feeds off our fears and obstructs our true vision. Never wander without intention. Intention keeps us grounded. When we understand the subconscious mind - use it with intention as a tool of awakening as opposed to a distraction from reality - then and only then do we begin to harness the first tool necessary for reintegration of the soul and body, the subconscious mind.

When we come to Earth, we all suffer **soul amnesia**. The human plane is so dense that our bodies and physical minds have a hard time seeing and feeling our souls. Part of this disconnection is a survival skill. Especially as a child, seeing and being distracted by beings of other dimensions can keep us very unattached from our reality and goals on Earth. We can break that cycle through knowledge and understanding. For example, I myself suffered as a child because I was not aware of this. I didn't have assistance. But, my own children have never had to ignore their soul selves for survival as I was able to teach and guide them early on. In that way, we have broken another barrier and chain limiting our family line. Even fear of death is part of the programming. If we knew where we went when we died, we would no longer fear death. We have been energetically written to try to survive. It is an innate biological reaction woven into our programs, so we don't quit the hard lessons we take on. Without the fear of death, our human forms have very little incentive to keep moving forward. If we quit our lesson, then the planning and evolution connected to it are irrelevant, stunting our evolution.

As we learn to control and utilize our subconscious mind, we begin to open up new aspects of ourselves. This is where our gifts come into play.

Many of us have gifts and they look very different depending on the soul group, and individual. Our gifts are embedded in our soul code. They open as we evolve past certain milestones in our lives, an intricately written trigger and response mechanism. "When you learn self-control, you may open this gift." Or "when you have achieved life 432, you may open this gift." If we don't understand our gifts, then we feel like we have no control over what's happening; something beautiful can turn into one of the worst things that has happened to us. For example, if your gift is to sense the emotions of those around you, you would also need to be able to flush these emotions so that they don't linger in your own emotional body. Not knowing this and how to do it means that you are absorbing the emotions of those around you and unintentionally allowing emotional debris into your own emotional body and reality. This can and will manifest into dangerous physical ailments and a doctor may medically label and medicate this. Just like that, your gift becomes your prison.

I myself have guides come forth as past versions of myself. Please note that although time does not exist outside of Earth, I use time related terms to clarify information here where time does exist. My past lives can teach and guide me, because they are not restricted to a timeline. Time is a creation of humans because our bodies deteriorate and because our human mind, much like a computer, processes information in a sequential linear system; time.

Our souls are not male nor are they female. Our souls don't have genitals. Genitals are only needed for human reproduction, so they are not necessary at soul level. We attribute "male" or "female" qualities to souls based on how they sound and present themselves. For example, if they have a low **vibrational tone** (or voice), we as humans may associate that characteristic with the masculine traits of Earth. A guide and soul can take on any form. They usually come to us in a form we will recognize, such as deceased relatives or a form we will understand. Some guides take on forms particular to their soul groups. For example, celestial bodies look like bubbles with galaxies in them. Grays look like typical "aliens". Angels look like, well, angels. Our past lives may also come forward in their past life "skins" or image, just as any soul has that ability.

This brings me to my point: how can our past lives be guides to our current life? We all have a higher-self. **Higher-self** is like mother/father soul or master puppeteer of your consecutive lives here on Earth. Because time is nonexistent off Earth, higher-self "parents" all your lives at the same time. When we decide as souls that we want to take on the "school" of Earth, we begin planning our lives, missions, and journey. We do this planning in the Akashic Realm. Although most lives are meticulously planned, we do have emergency drop ins, re-runs, and sometimes re-planned lives. This means that nothing is truly set in stone until you have physically worked through it. Free will still plays a large factor in our physical experience. Regardless of all the meticulous pre-birth planning, we are still very involved in our future. One choice can and will truly alter our experience. Usually when psychics see the future, they see the path of least resistance. That means based of the decisions you are making today; this future is the most likely future. Because I connect and deliver information through the Akashic Realm, I say "You have multiple choices written out. Choice A looks like this. Choice B looks like this, and choice C looks like this. Which one is more favorable to you? Where do you want to see yourself and how much work are you willing to put into this?"

There are multiple levels of the Akashic Realm and the Akashic Realm is highly protected because of the information it contains. Life planning in the realm is open to all higher-self souls who wish to come in and plan their own lives. They do this with a large group of advisors, soul family members and soul group members. Because no one lives their life in complete solitude, this is not a singular process. Planning is always done with an audience of souls who believe they can play a part in this plan, like an audition. The only time a soul would face the committee alone is if they are coming from Earth to recreate, change, or alter their experience. **Deja vu** is simply a reminder that you are on one of the planned paths that you created in the Akashic Realm. Your plan is simply rerunning itself in your soul memory system.

Higher-self may send out 632 fractions of itself as animals, **elementals** (elementals are fairies or, water spirits, fire spirits, earth spirits, wind spirits and orbs etc.), as well as humans, to live consecutive lives at the same time all reporting back to higher-self regularly. Your fractionized soul that resides in this current body **astral travel**s frequently to retrieve information and study or learn in spirit. They accomplish their own missions and goals while you sleep and bring back the information or new downloads for the unconscious mind. We need to physically connect the conscious mind to this process through soul discovery and awareness. Many times, you don't remember these trips because we fear what we don't understand so we are unaware and disconnected from the soul memories during the astral travels. If you don't consciously know what is happening, this could stress our conscious mind right out of sleep. Sleep is vital to our human form, so it's something souls don't like to mess with. If you are not consciously aware, it is simply not time just yet. Many people confuse these missions, memories, and astral travels with **dreams**. As you evolve, you can and will become a part of the process.

Because some of the memories from our astral travels are confused as dreams, recording your dreams is very important to your spiritual growth and is a great tool in self-discovery. Many times, our dreams represent our greatest fears and desires. They represent our subconscious memories, thoughts, soul missions, travels, and lessons. This knowledge is a great tool for connection and growth.

Our higher-self will also take many fragments of self and say something like "Here is an angry clump of me. I will send it down into these kinds of lives so that these fragments of me may resolve our anger." Then they may say "This mission will take about 162 lives to resolve. So I will send 162 fragments to complete similar lessons and resolve this. Off to life planning you all go." In this way you are never an exact replica of your sister and brother lives. You will resonate to the lessons and blocks in those lives because they are a part of your higher-self and energetic body. But you will have soul fragments, or sister/brother souls, that are nothing like you even playing your exact opposite. When your fragments of higher-self go into life planning, they begin creating the story to accomplish their lesson and resolve their undesirable traits. In this way, many lessons can be similar to others. For example, we all have a life in which we have been unfaithful and a life in which we have been cheated on. We all have a life where we have lost a child or loved one. If you know something in this life, it is because you have experienced it first hand in another fragment of higher-self. If you know violence is wrong, it is because you have experienced violence first hand in this life or another. Those who continue to be violent in this life are at that place in their own evolution where they are learning and experiencing violence first hand. If you know love, it is because you have experienced it. That deep yearning for an intense love connection that goes beyond the physical, is the memory of real love from another life. If you are still yearning, this is a cue that it is out there, and you have not achieved it.

We do "study abroad" and choose lives on other planets, dimensions, constellations but this is actually quite rare, just as studying abroad here on earth is not the norm. Generally, most people choose to study at home or in their country; it is the same with these incarnations. Most souls choose to master their home first. Earth *is* one of the hardest locations to incarnate. That being said, most of us stay here. Earth is simply the place to be at the moment because there are so many lessons still available and it is still inhabitable. Inhabitable planets are a rarity in the multiverse. At the moment, Earth is the "college" that will give you the most experiences and lessons for your higher-self. Our bodies are crafted by our soul groups **source** or creator and the energetic weavers of our reality (or **life weavers and programmers**) for the planet in which we inhabit. Different soul groups in other dimensions have different creators, or source. Billions of years from now, if Earth is uninhabitable and we (all of the soul groups currently inhabiting Earth) find another planet, our creators and the weavers will team up with the inhabitable planets creator and get to work establishing life forms that are congruent to the chemical and biological makeup of that planet. This may start out as simple life forms as we build the codes and try to understand the planets composition, they get more complex overtime as or understanding of the chemical and matter of the planet evolve. This process is essentially the theory of evolution. Yes, we evolve in the physical form – but the energy in the inhabitable planet is manipulated by creators slowly establishing life and evolving the program to take on soul fragments. CREATORS. Not singular. An inhabitable planet doesn't last long with one creator. We are all granted access and travel – as long as we can build the program appropriate to connect our soul to the biological makeup of the planet we wish to inhabit. This can take millions of years of trial and error.

Weavers, simply put, are the energetic - behind the scene - workers that create our current reality. They weave together everything our five senses can experience. There are levels of weavers. **Level 1 weavers** work in our day to day lives, in our step by step realities. When we make a decision, they get to work creating that reality. **Level 2 weavers** drop in larger programs to the fabric of our reality. For example, you choose to go to college. Level 1 weavers would begin creating the connections to people, places and things that bring the likelihood of college closer. Then when college is a reality, level two weavers would drop in the college "program". This college program will look the same to everyone attending that college, but the personal path that brought you there is unique to everyone. Then we have **level 3 weavers**. They are responsible for the larger aspects of our reality: weather, global events, and world issues. Level three weavers work under the planet's creator.

Our Akashic life maps have multiple paths written on them. Millions of branches. Millions of decisions and "what ifs". We then have other souls that volunteer to play certain positions in our lives as it is congruent to their own journey and goals. We even plan and write in things to keep us on track and push us back to our plan if we become distracted. If a soul fails to follow the plan the soul can still pick up lessons, but the specific lessons in the plan will be considered failed and higher-self will have to restart that mission planning with the same soul fragment until they get the lesson right and work through the goals as intended. These fragments will incarnate into very similar situations as the "failed" incarnation and usually with the same family and soul family. Once you have failed a life you bring all of the energetic and emotional debris of the first life back with you. This can be really thick and difficult to bear. Understand, these burned habits are now on life 2, sometimes life 3 and 4! Because they are repeated so many times, these can be the hardest obstructions we face. This is what we call **ancestral karma**. We live the same life, in the same family, as different relatives until we break the cycle and learn our lesson. Learning our lesson allows us to finally escape and separate from the blocks, themes, and cycles. There are billions and trillions of lives to choose from. No one is obligated to choose a part or role. They do so out of free will. Regardless of all this planning, humans also have free will. People may ditch the plan day one at birth or get stuck on a lesson at 23 that derails their long-term goals.

If you are still with me at this point, you understand that our subconscious mind is at all times connected to all of our consecutive lives through higher-self. Meaning, the information and wisdom from these lives is available to us, if we learn to connect to our higher-self. How does this connection begin and strengthen? First with the understanding, and then through meditation.

MEDITATION BACKGROUND INFORMATION:

Everything is energy. It's a scientific fact that everything that surrounds us is energy, even what is beyond our human senses. So it would make sense that certain energies are better for certain connections. **Chakras** are like energetic filing systems to our consecutive bodies. Chakras hold information of our emotional, physical, and spiritual bodies. I learned to read chakras from my guides and through the

Akashic Realm. It's important to note that the majority of souls currently incarnated here on Earth have a chakra system, but some rare soul groups do not. They simply are not created that way. I can still read their energy and information, but they may have a hard time connecting to the chakra guided meditations, sounds and terms because of their soul makeup.

Basic chakra information:

Root chakra (red)—foundation, structure, deep rooted trauma, childhood, abuse, feeling unsafe, issues grounding and connection to Earth

Sacral chakra (orange)—creation, creativity, sexuality, passion, balancing masculine and feminine, success, dance, movement, nurturing

Solar plexus (yellow)—what we radiate and bring to the world vs what we internalize. Digestion of our environment, energy and food. Self-esteem. Digestion issues.

Heart chakra (green)—guilt, forgiveness, love, empathy, healing

Throat (blue)—what I speak becomes me,

3rd eye (indigo)—how we see ourselves and the world. Ability to plan. Ability to see your worth. Self-image.

Crown (violet/white)—ability to know and connect. I am part of a whole. I am whole in my parts.

I always start at the root chakra because the root chakra is where we flush out our pain and negativity. The root chakra is also the first major chakra and connects us to Earth, important for our human experience. We have many more chakras that are not listed here, but these are the main ones I focus on during my readings. The surrounding chakras information come through the main chakras during readings. In this way, they are not ignored or lost. If we work the other chakras before the root, the root chakra will not be able to properly flush and dispose of the obstructions we loosened in the upper chakras. Because the root connects to Earth, it is where we absorb healing for our physical bodies. Earth also takes in and recycles the negative energy and obstructions from our body as part of the healthy root to earth connection. My gifts allow me to find past and future lives, spiritual gifts, blocks, obstructions and damage in the energetic chakra filing system. I also have the gift to heal, rewire and repair the zones of energy, or chakras. Sometimes we have a master gift with **gift guide**. A gift guide is usually a past version of ourselves that has already mastered that gift on its own. They might come through to remind us what we already learned. **Master gift** means that all your other chakras have gifts made to accentuate and accelerate the master gift. Sometimes the gift guide can be a deceased relative, sometimes it's a gifted master. Sometimes we have smaller fragments of one major gift in all chakras, spread out, and together they create one gift. This is different from the master gift. The master gift is so strong that it can alter the way we use and store energy in our chakras. It can alter our energetic filing system to make space for the larger program. Some people have more than one master gift and guide.

CATEGORIZING CHAKRA GIFTS:

Remember that each energetic system is completely unique, like a finger print.

Root chakra—connection to energy and earth, manipulation of energy, understanding herbs oils and plants, cooking, building

Sacral chakra—creation, balance, maternal/paternal gifts, dance, yoga, nurturer, absorbing emotions, art, music

Solar plexus—altering our energy and surroundings, reflecting others' lessons back to them, energetic downloads for others, projective healing, teaching, public presence, acting

Heart—Healing, emotional intuition and interpretation, understanding, judgment free zones, love, empathy, hands on healing, delivering codes and energy to others.

Throat—channeling, telepathy, power of spoken word, singing, connections to tones, knowledge of vibrational healing tools,

3rd eye—seeing past, present, future, souls, dimensions, energetic bodies, physical bodies, soul bodies, colors, animals, BS radar

Crown—Seer of souls, Seer of dimensions, channeling realms and realm energy

It would take a whole separate book to explain each gift - so this must be a general and short explanation.

Understanding your own gifts (a report I offer when you book via my website) and the chakras in which they lie will help you learn to unblock that chakra gift and open that energy. In general, most foods, crystals, elements that are in tune with our chakras will match the chakra color.

When we understand the energetic filing system we can focus on one energy or chakra at a time. Knowing that most lessons affect specific chakras, and knowing our chakras file our gifts, we can say "Your root is damaged. We need to open the past lives blocking your root and your root gifts." This gives us a focus and a plan clear with themes and direction. Without this plan and system, we will easily get overwhelmed trying to read 1,000 lives and their information, searching for those 3 obstructing lives for gifts that we think we might have and don't really understand.

This is also why I know I am never in competition with anyone. Our build and creation is deeply personal and intricate. No two souls are exactly alike. We all have our own structure, experiences, personalities, blocks and gifts that make us unique. This is also why copying others and following any single modality, religion and process will never help you open to your fullest potential and abundance. The only way to understand yourself, find abundance, and discover your full potential, is to reintegrate with the soul. Be true to yourself and take guidance from your higher-self and guides. This will look and feel different for everyone. So remember, you will never come into your full potential copying anyone else, you will only find it being true to you!

"You will fail 100% of the time you are not being TRUE to YOU."

Jessenia Nozzolillo

GUIDED MEDITATION BACKGROUND INFORMATION:

I would like to note that the information for this segment and the guided meditation that follows is available on YouTube in video format (or was at the creation of this book). Meditation is the magical answer to a lot of your questions. Through meditation we learn to disconnect the conscious worrying mind and connect the subconscious mind and find answers to a lot of your issues. We learn to give the subconscious mind purpose and direction, we learn to focus the subconscious so that it doesn't behave erratically. As we discussed earlier in the book, an untrained subconscious mind can and will act erratically and may cause you issues in your day to day life.

If we are not in control of our subconscious mind it will wander and cause havoc. Meditation has been proven to combat anxiety, depression and stress! This is especially important for "sensitives," some of which are psychics, mediums, empaths, tarot readers, and other gifted souls. Anyone who works in a healing field, such as in holistic healing or a medical field, will absorb energy from those around us. Some of these sensitives will absorb the energy of others at a much more debilitating rate than others, depending on your chakra gift system that we discuss later in the book. By picking up on other people's emotions, stress, anger, and other issues, we harm ourselves and don't function as we would when we are alone and in control of our energy.

It is also useful to learn how to control and properly use our gifts and learn to observe things from other perspectives. This helps us react more appropriately to our environment, including improving focus, problem solving, and creativity at work! More than just a good tool, it is necessary for empaths, psychics, mediums or readers and other gifted souls because being improperly grounded, unfocused, or not thoroughly open will drain you very quickly. It will also make your connections erratic. You may be picking up energy from someone not even in the room instead of accurately reading the energy of your client. This means you aren't properly grounded, open and focused.

When you use your gifts, you are opening them to all dimensions, all places, and all beings you've experienced at soul level. That is very hard to control. It can be very hard to pick specific information up and can often be very draining and very dangerous. When we do this erratically, we can lose sight of reality as it can become overwhelming for the human mind and state. Therefore we open to information over time, in progression. Performing a reading on anyone leaves an energy imprint on your own energetic field even if their energy is healthy and positive but picking up *negative* energy is more detrimental to our energetic field as it drains us. Negative or unhealthy energy tends to drain you like a leech. It can make you more negative and make it harder for you to process thoughts and emotions and to see clearly. It can even make it hard for you to heal yourself and is one of the ways we diminish our own willpower. Willpower is the ability to choose that which helps and nurtures us over what we crave. Many times, those who allow negativity into their environment lose so much of their own energy that they simply can't find the purpose in doing what soothes and is necessary for the soul, such as living a healthy lifestyle. **Lower level energy** requires food to thrive, and that food is you, so always be careful. So many people say, "If you don't allow negativity to seep into your existence then it doesn't matter who you surround yourself with." And that IS true, to a degree. Here is my example: A person who you know is no good for you, uses you, disrespects you and makes you feel like dirt daily asks, "Want to hang out?" You respond thinking, they suck but they aren't me. I'm bored. I have nothing else to do. Why not?

"Sure, let's hang."

"Sure, lets hang," IS allowing negativity into your space and environment. That is your verbal acceptance. You cannot heal the spaces and voids created by the negative, while still choosing them and verbally allowing them back into your environment. When you learn to defend and protect your soul, you can then go out into public and if you happen to pass a negative person or energy then they cannot seep into your soul. You didn't allow them in. You didn't create any verbal or energetic acceptance. Then it becomes true. So, many people are written to assist those who may be stuck in the lower level energies. The proper way to do this without finding yourself getting energetically abused and used is to establish your boundaries, time, and energetic exchange. Energetic exchange means they asked for help and are willing to give energy in return for assistance. What happens when people don't give energy to receive energy? It just means they aren't truly ready for healing. It means they want attention and not healing. Now, this doesn't always mean money. When I was first starting out, I had a woman pick flowers from the woods and wrap them for me. She walked to the woods, chose and wrapped flowers. That was her energetic exchange. Her vow to use the information wisely was her energetic promise that she was in fact invested in her own growth. This is important because this is what leaves a lot of healers highly depleted. I myself truly believed that my job and mission was to sacrifice myself and my energy for the healing of others. I didn't understand energetic exchange at the time. It was before all this information had become a part of my physical experience. Then my guides came through and said "If you sacrifice yourself and your energy, then you can only help a couple people who are not invested in helping themselves. You will get depleted and again fail your mission. OR – you can heal yourself, love yourself, take care of yourself. Make yourself a priority. When you make your healing and energy a priority, you have the energy, ability and health to reach millions." That was powerful to me as I understood that it was not selfish at all. Establishing and maintaining appropriate boundaries and energetic exchanges was simply a better way to reach, help, and assist more people. Also, establishing and maintaining appropriate energetic exchanges was in fact self-love and self-care.

If you have a bad grounding connection, or a bad connection to your higher-self - you may feel dizzy, confused, or tired. Some people sleep after reading others or connecting to higher-self. You can have a poor reaction regardless of how well you're connected or even if you do too many readings in one day. For example, I once performed 200 readings in one weekend. It didn't matter how well-connected I was, that number of readings is a lot for the human form. Especially for a new reader! Some other side effects of poor grounding or energetic exhaustion include headaches, negativity, close-mindedness toward others, and irritability. These are all examples of what can happen if you don't open appropriately or follow a good regimen, or even when you overwork yourself.

The number one question people ask me is, "How do I meditate? It's so boring. I can't shut my mind up. I can't stop thinking. Who could possibly stop thinking?"

Meditation is not intended to help you stop thinking. In my process, meditation is a system of shutting down the conscious mind so that your subconscious mind can take over. Our subconscious is what's connected to source, higher-self, and your guide/s (when properly trained) so meditating allows us to practice and establish this connection.

In the process, your connections become much stronger and clearer. Your meditation sessions become more enlightening and healing. Just like a muscle, the more you use the system the stronger it will get. The more you use this program, the easier it will be to flip that switch next time until eventually it's more just a thought. So as in all things, practice makes perfect.

Now let's talk about drugs. A lot of people use drugs or alcohol for this switch-flipping or because they think it will numb the pain of using gifts erratically OR help them to open their gifts. Substances like alcohol, crack, and heroin numb our receptors. People do suffer from addiction to these substances for other reasons as well. *Every* situation is incredibly unique, and we should never assume why someone might choose to use drugs and inhibitors. Other drugs or elements like cannabis, mushrooms, acid, and ayahuasca are used to help people shut off the conscious and open the subconscious. These substances offer just a temporary solution and they can be very hard to control. Deep and profound connections can be achieved without inhibitors if you just practice! I myself do not and have never used any of the inhibitors in my readings or meditations, but I don't judge those who do. I simply wanted to add that they are not necessary for profound connections.

Next, let's discuss food. Your 3rd eye is the chakra connected to the **pineal gland**. Small and highly sensitive to environmental factors, it allows you to more easily raise your vibration! Eating MORE raw fruits and vegetables, and LESS meat and dairy, junk food, sugary foods, and carbs will generally assist in cleansing and revamping this energy zone. Some foods have low vibrational energy. It is necessary to eat less of those foods when cleaning the pineal gland because the low vibrational energy foods work against and inhibit this very sensitive gland. An occasional treat is perfectly fine but eating too many of these dense foods will harm our digestive system (or solar plexus chakra) and cloud our third eye. Drinking fluoride-free water is necessary as it is believed that fluoride will burn right through your pineal gland. Now, that being said - this isn't the case for ALL soul groups, just most. Some soul groups need meat and the dense energetic foods because they derive their energy differently than the majority. In that case, this shows up on their reports. Their whole energetic body is created to absorb energy from their surroundings, which also includes energetically dense food.

The third eye is said to be the house of the soul, as the pineal gland develops around 7-8 weeks gestation. My guides have told me that this is when the soul arrives to the body. The pineal gland, although small and sensitive, must be kept clean and functioning if you wish to open yourself to source more freely. Sometimes we have a body, or baby with no soul planned to come through. These are what we experience as miscarriages before the 8th week of pregnancy. I only know because I had two myself and that is when my guides explained. Again, I'm not a doctor, just sharing what I have received in my soul connections.

We have already discussed expanding your energy for connections in the opening meditation process, I call this "**opening**" energy. Now it is time to discuss "**closing out**" our energy. Although we must numb the conscious mind to allow subconscious connections and information, an active sharp conscious mind is a survival tool while we are here on earth. If we never dimmed down the subconscious, we would constantly be overwhelmed with emotions, energies and beings from other dimensions and realms. We would feel overemotional and overstimulated. We would be at the mercy of others' emotions and actions. It would be nearly impossible to function daily. So, closing out your energy is necessary!

To close out your energy, imagine your collective healing energy collected into a spear and then send that spear to someone who needs healing, positivity, and growth. You can also use this energetic bubble to manifest change into your reality. Thank your guides and the souls who came forth to connect and guide you. Thank them for their energy and information. Say goodbye and disconnect to all those you have connected with. As you close out, imagine a pure white gold and silver waterfall cascading over you, removing any lingering energy, connections, and leeches. Finish your meditation with deep breathing and sage, palo santo, or another appropriate herb or resin with the energetic signature of cleaning energy and space. Pull your energy back into yourself and keep it tightly around you.

How and why is **grounding** important to your meditation session? If you are like me and have a very hard time grounding energy, try to wear red, brown, or black clothes and keep crystals of the same color. Red is the color of the root chakra and the foundation for your grounding system. Black is often the color associated with grounding and protection in some traditions. Black crystals and candles usually represent protection. Extending your root chakra through the ground like roots of a tree, an anchor, or seeds—whatever visual resonates with you- is just a fraction of properly grounding your energy. In my connections I have found that those who have issues grounding usually have trauma in one of their lives associated with the root, so sometimes grounding isn't your block, lack of healing is. The root chakra is the lowest major chakra closest to earth. We do have smaller chakras throughout our energetic body. The smaller chakras are energetically "lumped" together by theme. Meaning if one has a relevant gift or story, it will express itself through the closest major chakra. By properly opening and healing this chakra we allow the debris from the other chakras to properly flow back to Earth for filtration and recycling. So, a blocked root can be the source of other issues.

The kind of crystals you use really depend on what you're trying to accomplish. In this exercise, in which we will be learning how to connect to higher-self, stick to crystals that coordinate with your crown and third eye chakras. Clear quartz, selenite, herkimer, apophylite, amethyst, pyrite, and angel aura quartz are a just a few. Generally, though not always, purple and white or clear crystals are used for the crown and third eye chakras. Crystals have different mineral compositions and energies and thus may be good for healing chakras with a different color association, but in general, crystal colors will coordinate with the chakra. Many crystals resonate with more than one chakra. Additionally, and again in very general terms, choosing clothes or food in the color that matches a particular chakra can help you focus your energy to the chakra that needs assistance.

If you are someone who suffers from high anxiety or very negative thoughts, you might want to choose black tourmaline, obsidian, or hematite for your meditation sessions. They are the best crystals for absorbing negative energy as well as grounding and amplifying positive energy.

Angel aura quartz is a crystal I have chosen as a symbol of my practice for many reasons, but mostly because it's a crystal that amplifies and heals all chakras. It's all-over body, mind, and soul healing, much like my mission here on Earth, so it makes sense that it is the inspiration for my business theme. It is also a great crystal to have on you when you're struggling to cleanse and clear old trauma and energy. Angel

Aura is quartz crystal which has been bonded with platinum and silver, giving it a pastel-rainbow shimmer. The addition of metals amplifies its power and energy. I have always been drawn to metals, which also have healing, energetic and conduction properties.

Another crystal I use frequently is clear quartz, which is an amplifier. It will amplify your intentions and your energy and whatever it is you're trying to accomplish. It is also great for this particular meditation. Amethyst was one of my first favorites. It's like a mother healer. It's popular for its ability to ease anxiety and balance the crown and third eye chakra. Many healers and reiki practitioners use amethyst. Pyrite is also called fool's gold and is great for psychic abilities and connections. It also heals and repairs aura, blocks negativity and assists in all over releasing of negativity. It has also been known to assist in repeated debilitating patterns and behavior which is our intent in this guided meditation.

Some herbs that help connect the crown chakra include sandalwood, lavender, Palo Santo, frankincense, and sage. Herbs for the third eye include eyebright, jasmine, spearmint, star anise, passion flower.

The third eye and crown chakras are very important for self-discovery, growth, and self-healing, because through your crown chakra you are connected to source, higher-self, and our soul memory. Through our crown we can also connect to your guides and deceased loved ones. The third eye also houses the ability to see beyond our physical barriers and limitations. It allows us to see what we could be after we overcome our own obstacles, which is also very important to keep us driven. Opening your third eye and crown chakras will also allow divine energy from creator to flow through and repair any of the remaining chakras and blocks that we need removed.

You are not going to want to use all of this. What you do want to do is take notes on what resonates with you and your energy and find what compliments and assists you best. If I have done a chart for you and you see you have a lot of root trauma in your lives, then stick to things that nourish and heal the root chakra. After we have a suitable starting process and you have chosen that which compliments your energy, you can begin the actual opening meditation. I have a free meditation app on my phone that I love to use in accordance with my guided meditation called "Chakra Meditation". I also use noise cancelling headphones. I love my headphones because my life is crazy and chaotic. I have children and pets, something is always making noise. They can be distracting. Noise cancelling headphones were so important when first opening my energy.

Each chakra has a vibrational energy, sound, tone, and note. As I do my opening meditation I imagine the chakra I am working on opening with the tone in the app and change the tone to accommodate the chakra I am currently working on.

This is where the part "be silent and do nothing" comes in. That's impossible. Instead of being silent and doing nothing - or attempting to - I focus my energy and thoughts inward observing each chakra and what it has to teach me about myself. As I am focused on one particular chakra, I imagine the sound breaking up any negative disturbances, lingering connections, or leeches that may have accumulated in the area of focus. I always start at the root chakra by grounding myself, then work up to my crown for opening my energy to my guides.

As you work through your chakras, always pay attention to what comes up whether it be images, emotions, feelings, or memories. Many times, those are your strengths and weaknesses in that zone. At first it may just be a sensation or a color. Keep at it! As you continue this practice, things get more vibrant and more amazing! Each chakra houses a different theme. For example, the root chakra is a place where I see a lot of trauma established in this life and others. So, if you get a flashback from your childhood when things were not so great, understand that this memory is one of your blocks and something that is currently hurting you. Pause on that memory, absorb the message, and ask for assistance. Ask your angels and guides to come through and bring about healing and understanding to this situation. Ask them to help you release that pain and that trauma and help you find the lesson there. Then finally, ask them to take the pain. When you feel that that energy has been taken care of and worked through, you may move to the next chakra which is the sacral chakra. Once that one is complete, keep moving up and up until you have reached the crown chakra. The crown chakra is where we find and see our guides and deceased relatives. The guided meditation I added continues past that to our higher-self. When I get to the crown chakra, I see the lotus flower opening up allowing a beam of universal healing white light through my crown chakra. This waterfall of a beam travels all through my chakras, allowing healing, love, light, and clearing. It runs right through my legs out of my feet into the earth like anchors to earth. When I do this, I become a divine receptor and conduit between the universe and earth, never a source of energy, but a conductor of energy.

I am not judgmental or exclusive of anybody's beliefs. Whether you are searching to connect to God/gods/goddesses/deities/no god, I'm only using it as a terminology for saying that I am now one with the universe, one with Earth, one with my creator and that is the visual I want to express. That is something we are all connected to. Even is our creator is different, we have a stronger connection when we call in our creator, whomever that may be. We are all current residents of this universe and we are all current residents of this Earth, so we must call them in for guidance and connection. What terms you use and who you call upon truly depend on your belief system and who comes through for you. Be true to your beliefs but always stay open-minded. I myself had been tortured with religion most of my life as I was always taught that I would burn in hell if I ever did anything wrong. My family explored many beliefs as a child – all essentially different ways to express the same thing, that human bias had taken over the history of soul origins. With ego, we found a way to use fear and discrimination to taint our belief systems and subconscious information. This caused me to release the idea of religion and the **God** (the Catholic image of God) altogether because I truly didn't believe that this violent harmful behavior made sense. How father God would punish his children that way never resonated with me. That being said, I was very surprised when God and Jesus both came through in my connections. It was overwhelming being a non-believer having Jesus and God come to me the first time. Now I have gotten used to the strong connection and consider it a blessing. Never being Buddhist (in this life anyway!) I was also very surprised when Buddha came through to assist in the healing of a client. The experience was beautiful to say the least. I have also seen Greek Gods come through and make their involvement in this world known. So yes, once again, everyone's beliefs have some truth. Earth is a place of multiple creators and master souls.

When you connect and open your crown chakra, this is the place you call upon your own spiritual army. This is the place many people incorporate their personal belief system. This is truly unique to you and so you should do whatever works for you. Perhaps there's a planet you feel drawn to, perhaps there is an Arc Angel you look up to, perhaps you have a god or goddess you feel like you want to call upon. It's important to use what you believe and to follow your own belief system. Once you have anchored that connection you will call on your guides and you will call on your past relatives that are connected to the highest of vibrational energy and source. Never open yourself to just any dimension or any vibrational energy. Connecting to lower vibrational energy can be very dangerous for you and your own energy field. For example, I call on angels, guides, higher self, God, Buddha, and Hermes because these are beings that have come through to me in my readings. I'm sure my list will develop and grow as I continue to read. I appreciate their assistance and I appreciate the energy they use to help me connect and deliver healing messages to my clients.

Your own group of beings becomes your team. The energy and the process you use becomes your routine. I do recommend that you stick to the guided medication for a devoted 22 days before wandering and developing your own routine. It's imperative to build strong energetic bridges before we wander. This practice and system is created to keep us "safe" in our exploration of the subconscious. It's easy to get lost. I have never liked telling people what to believe and I think that this is a great process to figure it out yourself. Developing this strong connection will amplify your messages from higher-self and guides. Anyone who tells you to follow them blindly is looking for followers, not students. I truly believe that this process provides you the map to figure things out on your own through your own connections.

As you begin to open yourself regularly, you might get messages in your sleep and notice you wake up just knowing things you didn't really have the knowledge of or couldn't comprehend the day before. You'll see **synchronicities** in your life such as repeated numbers, messages, cards, notes from friends, text messages, and emails, and all of a sudden, they all kind of relate to what you're hearing, seeing and feeling. That's a way your guides say, "Yes! You understood, we got this!" We may also experience **downloads** and **upgrades** to our energetic code during large astrological shifts. This can make us feel confused, drained, exhausted and irritable. Let the downloads and upgrades settle. Drink plenty of water and rest. In a week or month, you will see you have new knowledge/abilities/understanding.

A great tool that I also use in addition to the free chakra app is Thomas Walker's flute CDs. I don't know him or have any affiliation with him, I just love his work. Similarly, Russ Jones is another extremely talented musician that I follow on Facebook. There is something about the energy and feeling you receive when you listen to this music that I find so nurturing and healing. This music resonates with me because it awakens my own inner shaman, or ShaWomen guide as I like to say. Also, YouTube has amazing resources and guided meditations! Use them to your benefit. This background information and the following guided meditation I created can both be found on my personal YouTube channel.

If you are one of the millions of people that has a hard time listening, focusing and cutting out the conscious mind while connected in your deep meditation, take notes! Take a piece of paper and write: "May my higher-self guide my hand and deliver a message that is true and accurate and healing." Write freely about whatever you hear, see, think, feel. At the end of your meditation you'll see that this "junk" probably makes sense! It's called **automatic writing**, and a lot of readers, psychics, and mediums use this as a tool for accepting messages.

GUIDED MEDIATION:

The audio version of this guided mediation can be found on my YouTube channel. All social media links can be found at the end of the book.

If the first time doesn't work, try, try again! Just as anything else you want to be good at, the more you try the more your body and soul will find ease in this transition.

Today what I want to share with you is a visual for a guided meditation to connecting with higher-self.

To prepare, I always burn a little sage and Palo Santo. I like to have all the elements with me: water, earth, air, and fire. To represent these elements, I have a glass of water and a burning candle. As air is all around us, it needs no further representation. Keeping this in mind, I do share my gratitude for the air's presence in my process. I recommend having crystals to assist your mission during meditation. I have a variety of crystals I use daily. If you have some, gather them beforehand.

I like to start barefoot and on earth or earthly elements. My floors are all wood so that's easy for me. It helps me when visualizing my grounding technique.

In this visual, healing water overcomes the chakra or energy zone we are focusing on. As we zone in on one chakra, you may notice images, memories, feelings, or colors. These are blocks and issues to address in this zone or area. Acknowledge these images, blocks and visions but as the water begins to take over the chakra, release the image and memory to earth and your guides for healing and repair. The tone you will be hearing in the background of each section is specifically designed to work each individual chakra.

Ok, let's begin.

"Choose a comfortable chair if you are inside. If you're outside the ground works well. If in a chair plant both feet evenly on the floor. Straighten your back and shoulders, find your posture. Keep your spine straight while finding a comfortable relaxed position. Place your hands comfortably around you.

Let's begin at the toes. Feel the tingling in your toes releasing any stress and discomfort. Stretch the feet and legs, gently roll the ankles. Now settle them in to a nice place and allow the tingling to awaken the foot chakras at the center of the feet. Feel the gears start to turn in the feet as they open allowing healing vibrant earthly energy in for relaxation and healing.

Let that energy up through the feet, ankles, calves, knees, thighs. As the tingling sensation moves up it releases any discomfort, tension, pain. Gone. Let them find a place to rest and be comfortable. Moving that energy upward to the hips, feel them sinking heavily into your seat, relaxed, comfortable, loose.

Allow that tingling to move up the spine, strong but relaxed and loose allowing flow. Gently and slowly roll your shoulders finding a comfortable position. Feel the tingling flow down the arms, elbows, hands – bringing life to the hand chakras you feel a pulsing in your palms as they awaken. Roll your head gently loosening up the neck relieving and releasing any tension and stress. Find a comfortable position for the neck. Relax. Breath deeply and consciously in for 4, out for 4, and repeat. With every inhale we sink deeper and deeper into our state of relaxation. Deep in our comfort. Content. One with your environment. Ready for our opening meditation.

As we open this meditation today we ask for our guides to come forth and assist us in a safe and healing journey. We ask them to keep us shielded and protected with beings of the highest vibrational energy and light. We ask source to come forth and assist us and guide us. We are beings of light searching for healing and answers.

Start at the root chakra found right around the tailbone. Imagine yourself absorbing the red energy from earth. Deep down in Earth's core this energy floods up like waves slowly coming to you to fill you and ground you. Allow it in but remember its source. You are of Earth and Earth is your anchor. Holding onto you and protecting you undeniably. As the red energy swirls around your chakra, you may see memories, emotions, images. Address the visions, memories and energies. Take the lessons, leave the pain. The pain is a choice and we choose to leave that behind. We choose to send it off to mother nature to heal repair and recycle that energy. Flush out what no longer serves us and clean the energy of any obstacles like a powerful wave. They get consumed by the waves and destroyed. They are no longer a part of you as they return to Earth for filtration and care making space for stability, security, healing to take place and fill this space undeniably.

As the waves elevate they begin to turn orange. The orange represents the sacral chakra found right around your belly button. Let the orange energy do the same, flooding you with beautiful healing energy that overcomes the damage and repairs. Address the visions, memories and energies. Take the lessons, leave the pain. The pain is a choice and we choose to leave that behind. We choose to send it off to mother nature to heal repair and recycle that energy. See your worries and stress float away in the distance. They aren't allowed here anymore. Now we open the gates for emotional stability, passion, creativity and self-worth to fill this space. They are here to stay.

As the waves continue to rise they shine with brilliant yellow. Yellow floods you and overcomes you, filling up most of your rib cage area. This is the solar plexus. Imagine the healing waves cleaning and healing any blocks obstacles and pain you have lingering here. Acknowledge them then watch them float away in the distance. Anything that harms your health, anything that takes from your will power, anything that is causing addiction I release you. I don't need you. You are not good for me. Let them be swept away by the radiant yellow waves far beyond your reach. As they are swept away, we allow in personal power, will, energy, direction and happiness. We are who we choose to be. Our body is our temple. We will care for our body with care and determination.

Then the waves continue rising and you've reached the heart chakra. The heart is powerful place but not when blocked. When blocked it brings about pain and fear. Issues trusting and releasing. Feel the green waves overcome this area. Let it heal and repair and pain we have felt in the past, any heartache, deception, lies, mistrust. Gone. We will not let that harm us anymore. That is a choice and we choose to let go. We understand that holding on to these emotions and denying forgiveness only harms us and our heart chakra. We will not continue that self-destructive pattern anymore. Our heart chakra is our largest chakra and we choose to fill it with emotions and energy that will bring us healing, not harm. Let the green radiant waves remove any remaining negativity and anger from this area. Let the waves sweep them away to Earth. They are on their way for Earth's repair. Out of reach. As this area heals, fill the heart chakra with love, forgiveness, compassion, understanding and trust. Allow it to radiate all over you. The energy is yours for healing self and yours for giving healing to others. A green cocoon covering you from top to bottom. Healing your body and aura. Guiding you through love and light.

As we continue the waves upward they turn a brilliant blue. The waves are small yet powerful. The energy heals and repairs this area. You find your voice here in the throat chakra. You learn to say what you want. Scream over the ocean "I am......., I want......., I will......." what do you hear the throat chakra saying for you? Let those waves take away anything that stands in the path of your "AM WANT and WILL," let your throat speak the truth and protect you from those who wish you harm. What follows I AM follows you. Never use these powerful words for damage, use them for love, compassion, guidance and healing. I am driven. I am connected. I am thoughtful. I am radiant. I am capable. I am… whoever I choose to be.

Let's rise the waves up to the third eye. Here you will find the waves are a beautiful amethyst color. They are magnificent and vibrant. Speckles of gold. The specks start accumulating right on your forehead in the center. They start creating a shape and eyelids. Now eyelashes. Ask this golden energy to open this eye and bring you healing. Feel the tingling in the area and the golden flecks work to open your eye allowing you the vision we are all capable of. What do you see here? What does your future have in store for you? You are a clear vessel of communication and an unbiased receiver of divine messages. Allow yourself to truly see.

As the waves move up they flood us in a vibrant white and silver and gold glitter. They burst and overflow through our crown chakra. We feel the petals of the lotus begin to open one by one as the energy floods out of us through our crown. One by one the gentle lotus flower opens on top of your head. Feel the tingling of the energy working the area. Feel the vibrancy of diving light peeking through. When all the petals are opened, feel the beam of white light traveling upwards and out of your crown. See this light travel up and through the heavens like a divine rope connecting you to the universe and still anchored to Earth. The crown is now open allowing this miraculous white…. gold…. silver beam to heal us and fill us with its radiance. Here you may see your guides, celestial beings and deceased relatives. Connect to them, receive messages. Thank them for coming through. Thank them for their guidance. They are always here in this area. Always with us.

Now…. let's find out what's at the source of your beam. Slowly follow that white light up. Through the clouds. Past the sun. Through the cosmos. See yourself there, higher-self. The grand puppeteer. Higher-self gently and lovingly holding all the beams of light from your collective lives and collective selves. Tell your master-self, "Please keep me connected to the information I need. Please help guide me consciously and subconsciously. Please be with me and remain close, I need guidance. I want to see, hear, feel, love, speak more clearly and through love and light." Begin to receive message from higher self.

Now is the time to ask higher-self questions that maybe ailing you. As you ask, higher-self pulls down a screen. On the screen your answers play out like vivid images. You see your purpose, your life, your future come through. Ask a question.

Why is this person in my life? Will this situation get better? How will I overcome this trouble? What have we planned for me? What is my mission? Give me the tools and healing I need to accomplish my mission on this life with dignity and love.

When you have finished your communications thank higher-self. Release your connection to higher-self. Follow the beam of light back down, feel yourself slowly descend the cosmos, the stars, the sky, the clouds. Slowly following that beam of light back to earth and back to your body. This information is yours to keep and use. This information is one with you. One for growth.

Thank your guides for assisting you on your adventure and keeping you safe. Feel the beam retracting and getting smaller and you close out your energy. Keep the healing. Keep the love and the peace. Use it for growth. Use it for assisting yourself and the ones you love today.

Thank you for being with me during this and Namaste."

Chapter 3

The Soul's Mission

―∽⌒⌒⌒∽―

Beyond simply understanding and connecting to higher-self, we need to understand why this is important and *necessary*. Connecting to higher-self is the next step in soul reintegration. Humans are not their souls. Humans are a product of their raising, environment, and education. Until we reconnect to soul, we are at the mercy of our physical understandings. Our soul waits, sometimes not very patiently, for us to open and understand this. When we do—that is when we find change. Our physical limitations can now be breached. Many see this as **manifestation**. Once we understand our souls, we can see our physical limitations and blocks. Readers who read the physical body are reading physical disturbances, lower level energies, jealousy, fear, and anger. If we connect to our higher-self, we are connecting to their soul not their physical body, thus we don't take in and retain their physical energy and ailments. Those who are made to only read physical bodies have built-in systems to shed what they pick up. People who stay on lower level readings and energies will see all the negativity first. These are readers that quickly jump to the conclusion that you are cursed or have attachments and demons. Although it can happen it is incredibly rare! They see all the negativity and sometimes that may look like an energetic attachment that they confuse with an entity.

This brings me to another point. Never let just anyone read you. Be picky about who you allow into your energy! I see it all the time. People will let anyone in; and anyone whose energy comes into contact with yours can linger in your energetic field. As we remove those blocks, we remove restrictions and false limiting beliefs, structures, and thoughts. We release our limits and boundaries and reconnect to soul. It is essentially removing the boundaries and walls from what's keeping us from what we want, allowing us to manifest at a much higher rate. I myself have been disappointed by many people because I see souls, and I expected people to react and behave from the soul. But they rarely do. Most people react from their "human condition". This means that a beautiful all-knowing connected soul may still have a detached human body. Treating that human like that soul will always lead to misguidance. People are exactly who they prove to be on this physical plane, until they awaken to their soul - soul reintegration.

When someone is ready, they come and find assistance. They are drawn to a master, teacher, modality, religion because they have awoken and crave deeper understanding. Knowledge, evolution, and spiritual connections can never be forced; one must seek the information on their own. Pushing and forcing others into your beliefs will always steer you wrong. It's a waste of your own energy and it's an intrusion of others' missions and processes. We do not judge a child for being two years old, similarly we should understand that everyone is on their own path, learning at their own rate, and we need to respect their rate. Most of us have anywhere from one to 1,000 or more lives! Judging someone on what they are going through in this life is really narrowing your own thought process and again creating and establishing a limited belief system in yourself. The judgments you project, are boundaries you accept.

Where was judgment born? **Ancient souls**, or the **ancient ones**, were the first souls to find and incarnate on Earth. Many of the soul groups that currently inhabit earth are considered ancient, especially in comparison to the newer Earth souls. Many of them where wanderers of the multiverse, creators of their own smaller soul groups, souls looking for refuge, fleeing war torn planets, fleeing vicious creators, fleeing dead planets and so forth. They were, essentially, loners or small groups working on their own to figure out the human process for themselves or their smaller soul groups. With little resources and limited interconnected relationships to other soul groups, they used judgment as a form of punishment for the unfavorable human traits they wished would cease. Their souls and bodies where so disconnected, they weren't sure how to deal with "misbehaving humans" let alone understand humans and their complex human emotions. This created a complicated issue. This issue essentially being how do we remove "unfavorable" decisions and characteristics of the human experience so that we can continue the evolutionary process, if they keep suffering soul amnesia? How do we change this without judgment and punishment? The Angelic Trials essentially changed this whole process.

Earth's atmosphere is incredibly dense. It is a rare consistency in the cosmos. This dense atmosphere amplifies the five senses and it also amplifies the emotional body. In this way, we can see how it's easy to get lost in this dense human experience where everything is so amplified and distracting. Although there are billions of soul groups, only the ones that have created a program compatible to Earth's human form and Earth's atmosphere and can incarnate here. The ancients where composed of the first of those soul groups. They were from all over the multiverse and every soul group is structured differently. Angelic souls are natural healers because they are structured as such. They are naturally not aggressive, they naturally avoid pain and punishment. They are delicate in energy and presence. **Angels** are a soul group of their own. They began by observing the ancient's incarnations. They were fascinated with human life and came in at soul level as **Guardian**

Angels because they loved to assist, heal and guide humans out of their "stubborn behavior". In this version, they look like apparitions with wings.

Earth's atmosphere is so thick it causes soul amnesia and soul disconnect. Many of us simply can't hear or communicate with our soul. Angels believed they would be more helpful in minimizing this issue by assisting and guiding humans in the flesh. This was one of many reasons in their decision to begin the incarnation process. This required they create their own soul group program. When that was complete, the bravest and strongest and most evolved of the Angelic souls came in (note that this didn't include Arc Angels or Angelic master souls). Now what happened next changed the world, multiverse, soul healing process, judgment, life as we know it. Angels surprisingly also suffered soul amnesia and soul disconnect. They truly believed they were above this "human condition" because of their human studies and soul makeup. But no, incarnated Angels did "bad" human things! They drank, they had anger, they hurt the ones they love, they lost themselves in the human form. Some more extreme than others. Lucifer was notorious in his life on Earth and became the prime and extreme example of what happens when **fallen Angels** (or incarnated angels) lose themselves to the "human condition". He lost the most of his Angelic connection while in human form. So much so, that he created a legacy with Earths people. The human senses became his addiction. He was gorgeous, loved the feeling of lust, love, temptation, dominance and sex. The amplified senses were too tempting for him. He truly became immersed in all of Earths distractions. You see, we use to fully immerse the soul into our physical vessel. This was a lot for the human body and many times the ego connected (if you recall the lesson about ego earlier on) was too much to bear. We became violent and aggressive. We fought one another. We ranked ourselves and others, we became aggressive and domineering. Our ego program simply too much for our human body to bear.

All the first fallen Angels where then put on trial in a huge interdimensional event. This event was called the **Angelic Trials** in which I had front row seats. Grand council, composed of elite souls, Ascended Masters and God, had to decide how and if the incarnated Angels would be punished. During the trials, the fallen Angels where shown their behavior and spoke about the deep disconnect they experienced when entering Earths thick atmosphere in human form. They compared it to being asleep and unaware. The grand jury decided that punishment and judgment was in fact unjust - but knew something had to be done.

The conundrum brought the grand council into a shift—birthing the system we use today. They moved into a multi-incarnation/evolutionary process of healing and reprogramming the physical body to be better adapted with the soul through layers or lives here on Earth. This new system meant, our higher-self would always be available to check on us through our incarnations and we would take smaller fragments of higher-self into our incarnations splitting the lessons up into many lives. So our higher-self is held accountable and always connected, but the fragments of higher-self have less power to "ruining things" for the collective when suffering soul amnesia. The obstructive lives become easier to heal and repair as we continue our soul evolution. Because of this, we have moved out of judgment and punishment and into repair, healing and upgrades. Every life we have is a new programmed layer, our goal being the full soul to body connection or program. As we work through our lives, we develop our layered programming and become stronger and more connected on Earth in a slower process of evolution and understanding. As opposed to the old way, where a large whole soul would come in, get lost in its ego, destroy its surroundings and then be punished on the other side by its peers and creator.

The first Angelic soul to accomplish this multi-life reprogramming was... drumroll... Jesus. Jesus is what Angelic souls aim to be in terms of physical goals. He is the embodiment of the Angelic soul groups standards for human evolution. As we evolve to that state, we would integrate with Jesus at soul level. As we master, we merge. So essentially, he is an Angelic being who has mastered his physical lives on Earth. The next coming of Jesus is any other incarnated Angelic soul who can accomplish the same. It is no easy feat! If you are of the Angelic soul group (or chose to merge into the group), at the mastery of your physical incarnations, Jesus binds you to his master soul through his "Jesus spark". Through this reintegration, you are bestowed his energy, soul memories and lessons. You become one. See, soul integration doesn't stop. We integrate the human form to the soul. Then soul to our higher-self. Then higher-self to our **master soul** or **ascended master,** in this example Jesus. Then to aspects of creator, this includes whatever cosmic DNA made up creator. Then we connect to our creator, in this example God (Jesus father). Then we merge with our universe, then to the multiverse and so forth until we have mastered oneness. Many people associate Jesus as male but that is simply because he presents himself in the image of his last incarnation when he was in fact male so that we may recognize him. Souls don't have genitals and genders.

Through this information, it's clear to see where so many human created religious beliefs and interpretations derived. Unfortunately, most of them are tainted with ego, human bias, negative emotion, hate, fear, greed, judgment, and exclusivity. Many, not all, of the ancient soul groups adopted this practice and system as they felt it would assist them in their incarnations. Some adopting the master soul and God, most adopting the evolutionary system with their own gods/goddesses/deities. Some soul groups began fleeing their more aggressive and violent gods to take refuge under Gods new system. In world history, this can be attributed to the disappearance of many ancient civilizations on Earth. They simply merged their soul groups for hope of less aggressive lives, fleeing punishment from their own gods eliminating some of the more "barbaric" practices of sacrifice and mass murder to appease the gods. Because of this, on this Earth, the angelic soul is in fact the majority as many merge to its soul group as we begin to understand each other more intricately. Its important to understand, this is not by force, but by choice. We do not become Angelic and sacrifice who we are, the Angelic Soul cluster grows to encompass us, our knowledge and who we are at soul level. This means we also bring in our own ascended masters and master souls when we merge. There are other soul clusters in the multiverse that are larger then the angelic soul cluster. They are not the biggest soul cluster out there. We must look at the grand picture and that is a multiverse experience with trillions of soul groups and millions of inhabitable planets working for the same goal, master and merge.

It also important to understand why we have the goals that we do. There is no good nor bad. It simply doesn't exist. We created this idea of good and bad because some choices bring us closer to our goals and some take us further away. If you think about is this way, **lower level energies**, negative or "bad" energies fed by ego are things that separate us. Killing someone, stealing, greed, hate, aggression, violence, self-destructive behavior. These are all actions that separate us from the collective. You cannot merge with your brother or sister if you still believe you are not one. This **lower vibrational energy** is what we wish to shed so that we may master and merge. All of the positive emotions that we attribute with **higher vibration energy** and "good" are emotions that bring us closer to the collective. Compassion, kindness, love, understanding, patience. They all bring us closer to the goals of merging. We understand our brothers and sisters' pain is also our pain. We see ourselves in others. We raise above the idea of separation and as we do, our soul group becomes stronger feeding the master merge goal. So even these soul groups that derive in "negative" or dark energy, cannot master and merge successfully in the long term. On this side of the multiverse, we merge as we combine our energy and those soul groups that thrive on negativity simply don't grow fast enough to keep up. They are too busy fighting each other to allow merging and mastery. This brings me to my next topic, when a planet or star is burned out, part of their energy implodes into a parallel universe where the goals are the exact and opposite of ours. The implosion creates a "dark" planet or star where chaos thrives. These are scene as black holes. Balance, even in the cosmos. Balance in the universe. Balance in the multiverse. What is "above", must exist "below". These beings and souls of these dimensions thrive in chaos.

The goals are opposite is every way. It is incredibly rare that they leak through the barriers that separate us as their energy and structure is also opposite. But it has happened in the past.

Even if you are not an Angelic soul and this master soul goal doesn't apply or resonate with you, this is vital information in explaining the reintegration process and the removal of judgment from our incarnations and life. Judgment is a thing of the past. Judging others and self can be the hardest block and restriction to rewrite as we are all essentially created in judgment and now have to come to terms with the integration and upgrade process. The reintegration process is still the same for the MAJORITY of souls and their higher-selves, master souls, ascended masters, gods/deities/goddesses and creators. Your soul group likely follows the same program, altered with their masters.

Now that we have discussed judgment and its origin, let's discuss how judgment continues to influence our daily obstacles on Earth. Everything is a lesson. Even how you react to others is a lesson. Why is this person triggering this response in me? What does that say about me? What can I learn from the process? How can I work through this to remove this trigger? For example, when I was a new mother, I would criticize anyone who didn't always consistently put their children first. This included anyone who traveled away from their kids, anyone who didn't sacrifice for their kids. I raised my children in this judgment and sacrifice for 7 years. I would say, "When they are older I will find love. When they are older I will start/finish this. When they are out of the house I can follow my dreams. They are what's important now. The rest of my life, husband, dreams, goals, education, spiritual development and even my safety will wait." One day I had to face my own judgments when my oldest daughter told me, "I don't want kids." I was shocked. I thought, "You can do as you wish. Whether or you have kids will be your choice. But, can I ask why?" She said to me "Because you put aside everything for us. You never accomplished any of your dreams. I don't want to sacrifice my dreams because I have kids."

Those words triggered a lesson in me I had yet to yearn. Yes, they hurt, but I brought light to the pain and chose to find understanding. Although my children are the reason I pushed for a higher education, a home, and opened my first business, they are also a lot of the reason why I justified putting everything else off until later in my life. I truly believed my judgment that you could only be a good parent through sacrifice, until I realized that my love through sacrifice taught my daughter the wrong lesson. Since then I have begun working on my purpose, mission and career. I have traveled and begun working on my goals. Now I think, "They are watching." My kids are watching and learning to follow their own dreams *while* loving and taking care of their families. They are learning that they can have more than one focus and passion. They are learning that we can do anything we set our minds to. They are learning that we are the creators of our own lives and destinies through the work we put in. And that's when I realized that my own judgments were extremely limiting and coming from a place of resentment. I unknowingly judged and resented others who knew how to balance the two when I could not. That was a place in me that was lacking. My judgment was simply judgment, an expression of my weakness and unfavorable human tendencies, not an understanding of their energy or character. Thus, I began the process of intentionally making a judgment a lesson. I suggest you do the same!

As we progress, you will be doing these guided meditations while unlocking soul traits, gifts, energies and aspects. You will be finding yourself out at soul level. You will definitely begin to see the world differently. The more self-work you do, the more questions you will have: that's where your spiritual guide team comes in and the guided meditation is created to make that connection to them clearer.

"Why do people say, 'I've come a long way,' like it's a reason to stop? Yes, you've come a long way. Congratulations! Imagine how much more you can accomplish if you just keep moving

forward? Humans are capable of amazing things, but only if they continue the fight to be better than the person they were yesterday. Continue the fight. Self-development is never done."

-Jessenia Nozzolillo

Chapter 4

Your Soul Story

"I don't know if I'm happy because I stopped giving a ---- what people say and think...

—OR—

If I stopped giving a ---- what people say and think because I was finally happy.

Either way, it's an amazing feeling and I only wish to help others find that kind of freedom, happiness and understanding within themselves."

-Jessenia Nozzolillo

This part of the course is about our soul origination and creation. This is the only section and report I offer that comes straight from Andrea Hess' Soul Realignment Modality in which I am a certified reader. To get more information on her system and process please visit her website.

In this section of the class, if you enrolled in the online course, you would have received your soul blueprint. The soul blueprint goes over soul origination and information such as soul traits and aspects which are specific to Andrea Hess' modality. For personalized soul blueprint report, please visit my website. All links can be found at the end of the book. I use this system to find soul origins and information about soul creation. During the second report we go through the current body and any obstructing past life experiences. Then in the final report we access the soul and soul gifts and go over any obstructions, blocks, or disturbances remaining in our gifts. This beautiful layered and analytical healing system is really an "energetic reconstruction" process. While searching and examining the layers of the chakras, aura, soul, emotional, and physical body, I can find, rewire, and heal energy through the layers creating the best version of you! Of course, you need to be involved. All the work I do is nothing unless the client allows the healing into their physical experience. You will also receive homework during the process. Free will is your strongest tool or weapon. You can easily will yourself out of healing by choosing to stay stuck in the same mental patterns even if the source of those patterns has been healed.

Humans are very stubborn beings that like staying in place. They like being comfortable and staying the same. It often takes a huge jolt or shock to their system to get them to choose healing and positive change and growth. Sometimes it takes being fired from a job to motivate a person to pursue their dreams. Sometimes it takes losing everything to finally see what was blinding you or keeping you stagnant. And, one of the most common catalysts to change is becoming spiritual after facing death. I myself was told I would face cancer if I didn't find the courage to face my own fears and "come out" into my full potential. This might seem like a punishment, but before "coming out" I was still very fearful of what others thought and still limiting myself and my beliefs. After they "warned" me about the trigger I had written into my story, I realized that yes, if I had cancer and was facing death I would view the whole world differently. I would view my time here differently. I would release the fears holding me back and limiting me. So, I decided to learn the lesson before the trigger.

Many people might hear that and think of this as a punishment. Knowing what I know now and being where I am, I completely see how I benefitted from being pushed, and I'm thankful I didn't wait until they, or I (higher-self) backed me into corner. This doesn't mean that all cancer is a trigger and chosen or pre-written. Every case is so unique, and I feel the need to stress that assumptions will not serve you in this topic, it is simply too vast of a subject. This is simply a choice I gave myself. Being an Akashic Reader I can see the option and stories we choose to shove our growth in a particular direction. The same happened with my business before this one. I was told it was time to change and time to close my last business and focus full-time on my spiritual path. I didn't listen. I dwelled, and I hid in my fears. Then I got a warning: either you choose to do it on your own with pride or I will force you out. I didn't know what this meant but I knew I didn't want that.

I spent a long time working on my reputation. I wanted it to be a choice, not forced. After closing the business on my own and making plans to move onto this path, I realized my license expired a week after I closed the business. So, I would have been operating illegally and would have gotten into trouble and had a forced closure. Thankfully I didn't wait. Thankfully I left on my own terms.

In my own connections to the Akashic Realm I have seen and heard of places Andrea Hess doesn't explain in her connections and dowsing process. Regardless, I find that her definitions are correct and accurate, even if we don't agree on terms. Just as the Akashic Realm is a database of energy and feeling, words can be different to our own energy. Just like here in Earth, many different words in different languages mean the same thing. Because we have different specialties in the Akashic Realm, I see a lot of what she doesn't see, and I use that information to create reports 2 and 3.

If someone decided to take the wild and scenic route and not follow their soul mission, birth chart, or path they may find they don't relate to the reading provided. That is incredibly rare and has only ever happened once in my work. In this case their report 2 and 3 are still accurate because those are done by examining the current energetic body and experience. It would not matter if the person completely shifted off their original chart. So, because your soul didn't plan it out and it's out of character it likely wouldn't show up in your soul or birth chart. Sometimes the person has experienced so much trauma that the soul report doesn't feel like them, simply because they have a lot of damage to repair. We are essentially showing them their fullest potential at soul level, when they find healing. I myself have found my own birth chart never related to me, until I healed from my own trauma and began living my life purpose and mission. I had to step into my chart. Now that I have healed and awakened my gifts, I can see how everything was always right on the money.

The purpose of this report is to energetically bring the soul back to its form at soul birth. We do this by repairing any leaks, tears and immense soul trauma that may have altered the soul. After this, we begin to dig into the other layers of the soul. Any questions specific to your report (if you had one) should be emailed directly to me in the time allotted after the report delivery.

I will use the remainder of this chapter to go over information I have channeled in my connections that is also necessary for understanding the soul-to-human reintegration process. I have only ever found one soul that was evil, what I usually see is not evil but disconnected humans who can behave in "evil" ways. As I explained before, our soul and human forms are very disconnected. Because of this disconnection, we can be susceptible to "evil" behavior in our incarnations. **Incarnations** aren't exactly real either since we don't really reincarnate. All our lives occur at the same time (for the most part) so it's technically considered **consecutive lives**, not incarnations. I will keep using the term incarnations so that I can be clear to our human perceptions of time and time related labels.

In our human form with our human limitations and disconnection we are susceptible to our human conditions, raising, education, and experiences. Because of this we may act selfish, violent, or disconnected. When we revert to higher-self we become all knowing and connected once again to our soul memory system. Many times, after a violent, aggressive life in which the soul fragment in question was the aggressor they will need time to heal, just like soul who played the victim needs time to heal. If you had played a difficult role, or were an oppressor, you may feel tremendous guilt and pain when crossing over. When crossing over and reconnecting to the soul memory, we understand our wrongs and the pain we caused the ones we love. Many times, these souls punish themselves. It's a system of self-torture fed by guilt. It looks like they are ripping themselves apart and burning out the rage and guilt from the painful life they experienced. This feels and looks like what we may consider "hell" and many souls have described this feeling as such. Eventually, these soul fragments come out of their self-induced guilt and pain and then enter the healing realm where they begin the healing process. Fire is a consumer, in dousing ourselves with fire at soul-level we allow the fire to consume the parts of us we no longer wish to carry forward. The rage, anger, guilt burned. We rip ourselves apart to make sure we have burned the remanence of that life in all our hidden nooks and crannies. On soul level, we don't need to worry about our physical bodies taking on damage, so the fire is used to burn the energetic parts of the traumatic experience they no longer wish to carry with them, so they may ascend past that lower vibrational energy and reconnect to higher-self. Sometimes a soul fragments pain from the "dark" life they lived becomes too intense and layered for healing, too dense for even fire. If a soul fragment has too many intense lives where they had painful experiences or hurt too many people repeatedly, a soul fragment might be too traumatized for healing. In a very rare case like this, your soul fragment would be imploded and then reborn on the other side of the multiverse. Into a new soul fragment and begin life as a "dark" soul thriving in chaos. No energy is ever lost, just like here on earth energy is recycled and repurposed. Energy cannot be destroyed or snuffed out, it can only change its form.

Reconnecting to your soul will allow you to see the highest meaning and understanding of all circumstances. Just like any other skill, this comes with practice. As you evolve your connection to your soul, shed your ego, and reintegrate the soul to self you will notice that your perspective shifts. At this rate, we no longer see people's actions as aggressive attacks but as mirrored images of their own personal insecurities. We no longer see our pain as pain, but as a lesson. We no longer see a headache as a headache, but as a block to our crown chakra. We no longer see our choices in this life as punishment, we see them as a plan. We are no longer the victims of our circumstances but the divine creators of our reality and circumstances. We no longer dwell in the physical events that created us because we understand the growth, lesson, and plan. It is a beautiful vision to share with the world and part of what drives me to do what I do. If we could all view the world through our soul eyes, we would experience this life in a completely different form. Truly open people understand that we are never done learning and if we are done learning we simply wouldn't be here on Earth.

Soul families are an interesting aspect I want to share. Everyone and their mother seem to have their own opinion of what soul mate, soul families, and twin flames mean. A soul family is a group of people with whom you incarnate frequently. Your soul family is usually around the same level as you energetically and in evolution. You may be from the same origin, but that's not a necessity. It's like your graduating class in high school. You all started the same year but some of you take a little longer to mature and some matured way faster and branched off to do their own thing. Soul mates are not twin flames. Soul mates can be mothers, fathers, uncles, brothers, sisters, best-friends, or even worst enemies. The reason for this is that soul-mates are technically members of our soul family. Your soul-family will continue to incarnate with us for multiple lives and missions. Sometimes these missions require playing the oppressor. We have all had to play an oppressor at some point in one of our past lives to challenge a loved one's growth. If we are coming to earth and need a lesson in which we need to be challenged by someone, many times our soul family will say "I love you so much, let me play that role because I know that I can control myself, but I hope you can forgive me when we return home."

Just because someone is soul family does *not* mean you have to accept and love them in this life after they played an oppressive role. Sometimes members of your soul family will simply not be good for you in this life and form. Sometimes you will not re-sync until you both return to soul-self and shed the skins and roles you played in this life. So, by all means, remove toxic people from your life regardless of their "soul relation" to you! Including soul-mates!

Soul mates are members of your soul family but *usually* with an emphasis or theme of friendship, love, compassion and support. Our soul mates are usually written in to challenge us into growth before our twin flame arrival. Because of this, soul mates can also represent difficult relationships and situations in our lives. We take on and accept themes with our soul family members. You might have a soul family member that will always play your challenger, or you might have one that will always play your supporter. There are millions of themes I've found in my own connections. Soul mates can even step in when a twin flame relationship is too damaged for healthy love in this life.

Soul group is a group of souls who came from the same place of origins. They may share a creator. They may share an origin story. They usually have similar soul structure and a similar energetic body. Some ancient souls denounced their creators and/or origin stories, in this case a soul group member may have been created from another source but adapted to a particular soul groups energetic structure and refers to themselves as a member of that soul group, for the most part.

Twin flames do not occur in every soul group, most but not all. They are the other energetic half of your higher-self. Someone you are currently working to merge and master with. They complete you in ways you didn't know you needed completing but just like everything else in our existence, that's not always black and white. Twin flames need to agree that they are ready for a relationship in this lifetime to be considered twin flames. For example, I counseled a couple who was not a twin flame connection only to find out that the male in the relationship disengaged his title at soul level because he was going to come into this life with disabilities, something they agreed to at soul level before incarnation, but which would make him an unhealthy partner to his twin flame in this life. After a lot of intense decision making and counseling, at soul level, they both agreed that they were ready for the complications and would rather reunite thus lighting up their title as twin flames regardless of the challenges that lie ahead.

Twin flames are not always perfect for each other. Sometimes one half of the puzzle may be suffering intense trauma from a past or current life and are simply not in a place to be healthy for anyone, not even themselves. They cannot be forced to heal, not even by their twin flame. They must find and seek healing on their own. The best thing you can do to assist a twin flame in healing is to separate yourself from the situation and heal yourself. As you begin to elevate your own energy - many times theirs will elevate as you are connected through higher-self. Physical separation is truly key. You cannot stay together and focus on your growth when they are damaged because your focus will always be on their healing and not your own. By damaged, I mean intense damage that is causing intense physical, emotional and spiritual harm. With the inappropriate and intrusive energetic focus on their healing, your energy will take over their vessel, depleting you and shoving their own energy out of their body. This energetic imbalance can happen to anyone we try to inappropriately assist, not just twin flames. The only way they can find growth is if they can focus their energy inward, and they can't do that when you have filled their vessel with your own energy and worry. Taking care of others is different. We're talking about intense situations where one partner is far more energetically involved in the healing of their partner, even if their partner has no intention to change. They will say they want to change, but they have no intention to do so. They also can't create and establish intention while you are eyeball deep in their energy. Keep that in mind. You have simply taken over their vessel so much that there is no longer space for their own growth and intention.

Many people encounter soul mate relationships in which they are happy enough and stay their whole lives. That's okay too! As I mentioned, some soul groups don't have twin flames so soul mates are essential. We may also choose not to incarnate without our twin meaning a soul mate is our best option. Sometimes people aren't ready to believe there may be a different/better relationship for them out there and choose to stay in a soul mate relationship. These relationships can be comfortable and loving and if you don't know what you are missing then it's easy to get stuck. That's your choice! No one can tell you what you are not ready to hear and we as humans can be blinded by our heart and fears. This is simply part of the human experience.

Soul mates can also take the place of a twin flame who isn't ready to perform in this life. This is a reason why we shouldn't remain stuck, even in twin flame relationships. Your options are limitless. If you are having a block to love it is usually a deep-rooted soul issue that's rejecting love on many levels rather than not having "found the right one." When we remove our blocks to love we call in our twin flames as we are connected and can pull them to us or vice versa. Again, if they are not healed, you may have a hard time pulling them forward even after your healing. In this case finding a loving soul mate replacement is possible!

We have many soul mate relationships sewn into our story to teach us lessons and growth before we reach our twin flame reunion. So even soul mates are a necessary part of the story. Because I also see past lives vividly, I can say that many times people confuse a soul mate whom they had passionate past life connections for a twin flame. This is a common issue because of the strong energetic connection throughout lives, especially if these past life relationships were sexual and passionate. It is a real and powerful connection. It will feel stronger than a "normal" soul mate relationship if you have these inappropriate past life connections leaking through. If this is the case, I can see this and remove this. This would feel like you have an energetic pull to the person and you can sense their emotions, feelings and energy, even if they aren't good for you and it never seems to work out. It is not a good feeling and can leave us feeling stuck on the wrong people and drained. Many times, these relationships are explosive. Many times, they end just as quickly as they began.

Our mission in our lives is to work toward **Oneness**. Oneness is all-connected understanding and unconditional love. It is the interconnected highest beings working together in cocreation and evolution as a flawless team of love and acceptance. Master and merge. So connected and understanding that we perceive ourselves as one. We learn here on Earth through physical experience and the mission of this physical experience is to remove all negative expressions of ego, obstructing emotions and blocks until we have learned and experienced enough to be one. Final integration, oneness full cycle from creation to creator. We are all working for the same goals. Just like you are a fragment of your higher-self, your higher-self is a fragment of master soul, master soul a fragment of source and yes, this "upward" connection continues through our universe and out! As we work to develop ourselves, we heal the collective whole. Therefore, we find profound healing and change when we look within. We are fragments of source. In understanding yourself at a deep level, you are essentially understanding and building your connection to source.

Once we mastered the Earth form, we began incarnating to different planets and dimensions to master those lessons brought forth. Earth isn't the only place to incarnate, but it is popular place right now as you can get "more bang for your buck." By that I mean that one can experiences a lot of challenges and obstacles and thus growth in a short period of time because of how complex Earth currently is. Compared to other dimensions or planets it is considered an "expedited evolution crash course" in many ways. **Realms** are not dimensions. For the most part a realm is a place created by master souls, not a place located within a god/goddess creator.

Some deities/gods/goddesses are created with cosmic DNA that may push them into categories of "punishment" and order. That may be their job, but even so they do this to keep order, not to judge and be exclusive. In that case, that is their job, not ours. Eventually these souls revert to the darkness as they flip to the other side of the barrier in the multiverse. That is simply where they thrive.

Karma is not a punishment. Karma does not run around cursing people for you. And no, contrary to popular belief, Karma is not a bitch. Karma is essentially an energetic paycheck that looks different for every life. For example, one might have had a life where they killed many people, and this creates an energetic karmic "negative" in their bank account. They then may choose to heal many to return the Karma and give back what they took in another life. In many ways it's a choice we make at soul level to create and maintain balance and order. You pay back the energy you take. Everything is equal and opposite in every way. So yes, even the highly evolved healer has had a life or 300 where they balanced that Karma and possibly hurt some people! Karma cannot be tampered with. It cannot be removed or altered by an outside source. It's a debt that must be paid. Some souls find ways to dump karma splitting it up to soul family members who AGREE to take parts of the karmatic debt fearing it may be too much for one soul to bear. Some people simply hold Karma so that a soul family member may live out their lives making smaller payments and not one large lump sum deposit that may be to aggressive for the soul at hand. Either way, it always gets paid.

We all incarnate from other soul groups, dimensions, universes. Very few humans are actual Earthly beings. When our mission is done here on Earth we will move to another planet or dimension, if we choose to continue our evolution. In many ways, we are all alien. There are also souls who are incarnated in alien bodies at this very moment! Many of us have lives, guides, soul family, and soul group origins connected to those current alien bodies at soul level. I say soul level because we have a lot of soul level connections that we are completely oblivious to in our physical bodies. Even if you came face-to-face with your alien soul group in an alien incarnation, they may not recognize you as one of their own. Either way, I do believe that's why they visit so much. They come to check on those soul family members who have chosen to "study abroad". Many of them are highly invested in their soul families and soul groups healing and evolutionary process. They also make their presence as guides known during my clients' reports.

The term "**old soul**" is a funny term to me because there is no time on the other side. Souls can be billions of years old and never incarnate. Soul "age" is not congruent to soul evolution. Much like here on Earth, if a human chooses not to go to school or college, it doesn't matter how old they are, they will be considered inexperienced. We might call it soul "street smarts". Some souls choose to never incarnate and maintain jobs in other realms at soul level. These jobs include gate keepers, life planners, child preppers, guides, and a whole bunch more! It is truly limitless. Souls who choose to incarnate can have around 1 to 1,000 or more lives. When we have accomplished all our Earth goals, we usually don't incarnate again but can choose to do so in order to help further evolve humanity or to assist a loved one.

Because of our many lives, healing deep intricate layers is necessary. Most healers offer surface healing. Surface healing without deep rooted healing is like cleaning water in a tank without changing the filter. Your energy will eventually muck it up again until you fix the deep-rooted issues and trauma of all your lives and reintegrate soul to self. A child might have fewer obstructing lives than an adult because sometimes our past life disturbances are awoken by **triggers** in our current life. Triggers can include struggle, relationships, and more. For example, if you had a bad experience with someone in a past life, meeting them in this life might bring up the trauma of that life. A child's experiences and connections are limited. In that way, they usually don't suffer too many obstructions at a young age. Exceptions to this are, being born with soul damage (report 1) and family karma. When we quickly reincarnated to complete our "family Karma" we bring with us our pain and weights. I explain this process more in the section on past lives.

When I first started opening to my higher-self, I told my guides I wanted to see it *all*. My guides told me that, "Even your perception of 'all' is a speck in the cosmos of what truly is. 'All' will never physically fit into the human mind, in the minds current programming."

Open your mind, there is so much more that is possible than is impossible. We instinctively, as humans want to categorize everything. This is a necessity for the physical brain structure but if we are not careful these categories become obstructions and then limits. Never let your need for categories and structure be a limitation to your physical understanding. Everything begins at a thought. You cannot create, paint, or plan anything in this world without physically seeing the creation first in the mind. This means that everything that's ever been, has first existed in thought. Make your thoughts valuable and work for you. Stay open minded. In my journey I've learned that more is true than is untrue. I have even listened to developmentally delayed individuals, and to difficult cases of those suffering psychosis and mental disorders talk about things that some would consider a rant. I have found some truth in all. Everyone's perception of their reality is true *to them* and says a lot about that person's vison, place, and evolution. There is knowledge in all perceptions. For example, I once heard someone talking about the movie *The Matrix* and say how we are all a part of this "manipulated life and game" and how we are "pawns to the system." To a point that is true. Life on earth can very much be a "game" or program run through the manipulation of pawns, or humans. It can accurately be viewed that way. However, it is your higher-self that manipulated and wrote the program. The program was created, initiated, and agreed upon by *you* at soul level to better understand yourself in all aspects including the physical aspect. Instead of brushing off their perspective, I think, "Where and in what way could this be true." This process of thinking has transformed my mental limitations into learning and discovery.

Lastly, if I fell and broke my arm three times, I would be scared. The next time I fell I might jump or flinch, maybe even grab my arm instinctually. That is a response from damage and the memory of pain. The same applies in spiritual development. If we remove a place and space of deep energetic trauma and you still react from the habit created by past damage, then you are again reminding the soul of the pain and circumstance that used to live in that reaction. Remember, as we train and remove these painful blocks and obstructions, you must also retrain the physical body to not "flinch" and react out of habit.

"You guide you. You obstruct you. You teach you. You change you. You is me. Me be we. We be one. One be us. Oneness."

-Jessenia Nozzolillo

Chapter 5

The Current Physical Body

This can be the hardest life to heal because it's our current life and form. We are very energetically tied to our current life and we are biased of our relationships and very solid in our perspectives. Breaking an energetic barrier is like an explosion or shell and it can be felt. Especially when we are breaking energetic barriers that relate to our current life and experience. Again, this comes from a place of first-hand understanding and channeling of the higher realms. I had to live this life to be able to teach others how to heal from their own trauma. I show my scars so that others may know to heal theirs.

Let's see...

I have suffered, firsthand the effects of loving someone with substance abuse issues more then once.

By five years old, I had already experienced homelessness and had been sexually assaulted more times than I could count.

At this time, my mother took off trying to find refuge for us, often spending sleepless nights in shelters, sleeping on floors or wherever we could find a warm loving "handout".

After we were placed in an apartment, we continued to hop around, moving about 15 times in the next 11 years.

I became pregnant with my first child at 17.

After suffering for many years in bad relationships and being raped by multiple people I had my second child at 21.

There were more abusive relationships.

Then comes the healing.

I enrolled in college. I found purpose. I found a mission. I discovered my gifts. I found healing. I broke the cycles. I worked my ass off. I created the home I always knew I wanted as a child.

Every day I find a way to give back. Even if it's not much. Every day, I still find something to be thankful about. I am thankful that I survived, *and* I am thankful that I overcame! I have grown into the woman I am today because I was persistent, because I fought hard, and because I never quit on my vision. I am not a victim. I am a warrior. Nothing can break me apart because my foundation is made of solid experience, persistence and passion. I didn't find healing, I built it from the ruins of my life. Once we awake to the reality that all of this "suffering" and all our experiences were simply created to mold and teach us, then we understand our purpose. The strongest healers take on the most aggressive lives so that they may better understand the rest of the population, so that they may have the tools necessary to assist others through compassion, love, and guidance. If everyone understood compassion no one would suffer. It's a mission we take on to better understand ourselves and others and we evolve through this world. Just like an athlete must endure tremendous physical pain as they rip and build muscles for their fitness goals, we too energetically do the same. The issue becomes when we don't release pain it will become suffering. Pain builds muscle, suffering is never needed. We must learn to feel then release again and again until we've retrained the physical body to make it a habit. In the end, we either allow ourselves to keep suffering and relive our pain, *or* we find release. Keep the lesson, release the pain. Heal.

"Magic is the ability to make what seems impossible a reality. We only discover new things because people have the bravery to chase the unknown, the vision to see what has not been seen. Be brave, chase the impossible - until it becomes possible- discover what magic really means. Everything we have created here on earth was first created in the mind."

-Jessenia Nozzolillo

This chapter is based off the information gathered in Akashic Report 2 of the 3 report healing system I offer and is also included in the purchase of the spiritual development class. In this report, I go over the chakras and the current body system. We may find ailments, obstructive past lives, and repeated cycles in our current life that need healing. I also find memories, childhood trauma, blocked memories, relationship lessons, and patterns that may have begun in past lives and found a way to continue into this life. Let's break this down so we can better understand their relevance to sorting and understanding our physical experience.

If you return to the beginning of simple life on earth, there was nothing but nature. Everything that has accumulated on Earth since then was a simple creation, a thought, an invention, curiosity, belief, vision, or *magic.* If we were to go back in time and tell an early human of the things we now have at our fingertips, they would look at us like we were crazy and ranting about a magical place that would never exist. At their level of perception, what we have accomplished would have been too far out of their mental grasp to comprehend. This brings me to my point: everything first begins in thought. Every creation, invention, or change first begins in the mind. Understanding this is imperative to self-growth and releasing blocks. If you find an obstructive thought pattern, understand it's your job to rewrite that obstructive pattern. If you get overwhelmed and think "impossible, that can't ever be accomplished" then simply start at step one again, with a positive thought "This is possible. I can and will accomplish whatever I set my mind to". You are the only one with that ability. You are the divine creator of your reality. Just as we are creations of Source, our grand creator. As much as I can tell you that you are a powerful, all-knowing soul simply taking on a human experience, you must believe it to reap the rewards and begin making change.

Understanding and immediately reacting to the emotional body will continue to keep the emotional body healed and unblocked. Do not let emotions and emotional cues linger. For example, I have had clients tell me, "I have felt blocked for 15 years," and I begin to investigate their life and record to see that 15 years ago they made a choice against their soul's intuition and encouragement. Let us say for the purpose of this example, that choice was to stay in a relationship that simply wasn't meant for them. Did you want to stay in this relationship? No. Did you feel it was right? No. Did you feel the push for better things? Yes. Those were all emotional cues calling you to remove the obstruction. Instead, most of us ignore the directions and simply keep suffering, clogging up our chakras with resentment, grief, lack of love, desire, depression and blocks to self-worth just to name a few. If she had listened to the cues of the emotional body, she would have less to repair. 15 years of ignoring the emotional body created 15 years of blocks we now have to energetically rewrite and remove. Pain can materialize from layered blocks and emotional cues we ignored. **Emotional intelligence** is the souls' way of helping the body learn new things and evolve. If it wasn't for emotional intelligence over a series of lifetimes humans would simply relive the same life every time with no recognition of their past lives and experiences. There would be no trigger for growth, no hint for energetic blocks as emotional expression. Very simply put, it is the building of energy that creates an emotion, the building of repressed emotion that can manifest into an **energetic block**. An ignored energetic block that manifest into ailments. We are supposed to take that built up energy and use it as a drive to heal, not dwell and obsess over it and allow it to continue hurting us. Sometimes, we have blocks we simply don't understand in this life. They were created in a different life and we were simply born with them. We are a lot more likely to simply accept these obstructions as a part of us. We assume that we must keep these blocks and limitations because they have always been a part of this body and form. Because of this, you and your higher-self will write a story into your current life to bring light to that block. For example, if the block is to love, you will keep having issues with love until you are so fed up with the reoccurring cycles that you seek change, knowledge and healing. Which is why you have come across me and this book, isn't it? Time for healing!

The emotional body is to remind you to stay on track, not to avoid situations all together. For example, someone might say, "I'll never do that again because I don't want to lose control," in a past or current life, but the lesson should have been to "practice self-control" and not avoid the situation altogether. So, once you can see and grasp these old useless thought patterns and past life emotional "memories" of what's holding you back, you can now begin to perceive things differently and use that emotional body's intelligence as a lesson instead of a hindrance.

Birth charts use astrology as an energetic mixing pot to give you the perfect recipe for your soul mission and goals. Everything necessary for your mission in this life is chosen and planned by you, or should I say higher-self to the exact minute of birth. Sometimes we still fail our mission even if the chart is perfect for the mission. But - it doesn't denounce the charts validity. It simply says you were more stubborn than your chart and need more of one thing or another to boost and encourage you MORE. I myself, was more stubborn than my chart and have failed many lives for this mission. Until, that is, they found the perfect flavors and spices in my birth chart that would encourage me out into my purpose and out of my stubborn behavior.

Life path numbers are connected to your birth chart because it can be found in your birthday. If your birthday is 8/28/1692 you would find your birth chart number by:

0+8= 8
2+8=10 / 1+0=1
1+6+9+2=18 / 1+8=9
Then: 8+1+9= 18 / 1+8= 9
Life path number =9

Then you could Google life path number 9 and see what comes up for you and what resonates to your energy. I love Google and used it for some things, especially when I was just beginning. Now certain numbers hold energetic themes to me because I began paying attention to the patterns and themes in my life when they appeared to me.

Your birth chart not only establishes the root of your being and structure for your soul mission in this life, it goes hand-in-hand with every single large shift in your life from birth to death. My guides directed me to get my birth chart read and, in the process,, I found Carol Cleary (clearycc@tds.net), she opened my eyes to the massive shifts engraved in your birth chart. You will see that every large shift in your life will be accentuated by the astrological soup in the cosmos that sets up and supports your shift needed at that time. For example, when I had met Carol I was just beginning to understand my mission. She saw that in the near future I was to awaken the healer within and take on a HUGE challenge. I myself thought I have always been a healer, I didn't realize there was any more to awaken and boy was I wrong. She saw the energy in my chart that "brewed" a "larger than life" mission or energy. She could see things I haven't seen myself by analyzing the cosmic soup in my birth date and how that would correspond to the upcoming shifts in my near future. And so, whenever I have huge energetic upgrades and shifts to my energy, they can be found in my birth chart. For example, I am a Leo. I didn't know there was any Aries in my birth chart or energy at all. I never paid attention to this aspect of myself, until I was hit by the Aries full moon. This full moon was the hardest shift I had ever gone through. I went to Carol to review my chart and came to find out I had 4 planets affected by Aries, a north node connected to Aries, and Jupiter in Aries. I can't tell you what any of that means, that's Carol's job. What I can tell you is, what I was feeling was the cosmic shift that was jolting and activating everything in my chart connected to Aries, and it was powerful! At one point I was reading a plum! I could see the whole growth and life of that plum, including every bug that touched it. That is also the last time I ate a plum.

Very rarely we have someone who does not relate to their soul charts or numbers. This is what I call "ditching the map and wandering in the woods". There's a lesson in wandering too but it means that your lesson will be very different from the lesson or plan directed during pre-birth planning in the Akashic Realm. Although your current life and gift report will match, you may find you don't relate to your birth chart or soul blueprint. Again, this is so very rare. I have only ever seen it once.

Setting energetic boundaries is essential to protect your own energy. I'll say it again, and again: Everything that triggers and harms you is because you have allowed it to do so or have a place in you that has made it possible. For example, I spent a lot of time in terrible relationships. I allowed this because my experience with men and standards for men were so low that I simply settled for and chose men who met my very low standards. If I had been confident, self-assured, knew what I wanted and what I should expect, I would have cut the relationships before they began. But I didn't, and that's all part of the learning process. Now I know. Now I simply don't let these experiences become comfortable in my life. People may try to step in and test me, or remind me of the lesson, I simply say nope, not today, not tomorrow, not ever.

Understanding and immediately reacting to the emotional body will continue to keep the emotional body healed and unblocked. For example, I missed my kids. I reworked my schedule to spend time with them. I didn't even have to think about it. I saw and felt the emotional body calling out, so I paused my time and life to nurture the emotional body so that it wouldn't create a block. If I had made excuses and kept pushing off the emotional body, it could have easily manifested into physical ailments or deeper energetic blocks and problems thus sabotaging my work and causing me to become irritable or angry and feel guilty regarding work and children. Do not let emotions and emotional cues linger. The longer they linger, the harder they are to remove.

I use the term "**blocks** to energy" a lot in this book. Let's break down what this means so we can better understand the term and feeling. A block - like everything else in our experience – is energy. A block specifically being energy that obstructs evolution and growth. Blocks can manifest in many ways. Sometimes they can present themselves as a reoccurring energetic pattern, memory, pain, people in your life, body aches, or it can feel like you have hit a wall in your progression and growth. It can also feel like you are completely lost and off track, even confused. It can look like physical ailments. It can look like emotional ailments. Blocks can take on many forms, but essentially blocks are anything that are inhibiting our growth and progression. You can feel, see, and remove blocks on your own. Because everything is energy, finding the root of the block helps us rework and reconstruct the energy of the block so that we may break it up and release it for good. Some blocks are more aggressive, some are small and hide deep. My guides tell me when it's time to address particular blocks to my energy. I will sit down, focus on the area, and analyze my own body. I feel out the pain or clump I'm picking up on. I then investigate this energy and analyze it to figure out its origins, then I release it and work through it accepting the lesson and releasing the pain. These blocks are easier to release during certain astrological events. For example, new moons are a great time to observe, set intention and create a plan of what needs healing. Full moons are a great time for shedding and re-growth. My guides have taken me as far back as my infancy in this life and many past lives to work through blocks and obstructing patterns.

Sometimes our energetic blocks in this life can manifest into other blocks like a chain reaction. We may see self-love and self-esteem manifest in our current life. We may remove that block and realize that this one block was inhibiting our progress at work, our relationships with others, how we presented ourselves, our personal relationships at home, and how we view ourselves. In this way, one block can essentially change all aspects of our life.

In this report we also find deep trauma in this life. Even if our mind cannot remember it, our energy will. Incidences as young as in the womb have come through in my connections, meaning that current life trauma can begin as early as the womb. Our experiences all have a purpose. You and your higher-self can and will shove you into a corner to force you into growth. Unfortunately, we as humans will get comfortable and there is no growth in comfort. We love to stay in place. Humans really do carry that "If it ain't broke don't fix it." mentality, for the most part. But, when you are done with this book, hopefully you will see waiting for it to be "broken" before we are energetically involved in the healing process is actually a lot harder than addressing the emotional body as we go along. When you are faced with a situation and backed into a corner, it's important to understand where it's coming from and what the situation has to teach us. If we don't understand and properly digest the situation, learn the lesson and flush the pain then the situation will keep lingering and will keep rerunning in this life and the next. This vicious cycle creates patterns of suffering, energetic blocks and what most people see as "family karma" or ancestral karma, as it continues to manifest in other lives.

We need to experience everything first hand. This is a physical world. We are here to understand and work through the human experience which is also a very physical experience. The human experience goes hand-in-hand with human emotion. This has its beautiful aspects such as sex, happiness, love, passion, and compassion. However, the physical human world also has its ugly attributes including hate, greed, violence, selfishness, and anger. The negative aspects are what we wish to flush from our Earthly experience and most of them are side effects of the soul versus body disconnection. Connecting the two, soul and body, helps us use and access our soul's knowledge in this thick atmosphere and strengthen our understanding. Although we are gifted a new perspective when we reconnect the soul and body, we still need to physically work through our lessons and blocks. It's important to keep in mind that this becomes much easier because you see your blocks and then correct a lot quicker than when disconnected - making the negative experiences very minimal. This only speaks for you. Unfortunately, there are plenty of disconnected people that surround us. So, although our awakening will not awaken them, it will give us better tools for understanding and removing those who haven't awoken to the soul. And yes, if you are a healer you will be drawn to help and assist those in their shift. Just remember that you are responsible for not depleting your energy, you are responsible for your boundaries and you are responsible for who you let take advantage of your kindness. Healer does not mean victim. Healer does not mean mortar. Healer does not mean you must sacrifice any of yourself to help others. That is not where we wish or need to be in our developmental process. The guided meditation I include in this book is a beautiful way of establishing a strong connection to earth and source so that you may heal without depleting your own energy. The stronger you are, the more people you can reach. That is part of my purpose, training healers to heal properly so that they stay healthy enough to heal thousands and, in the process, I reach millions, creating a tsunami of awakening.

As I mentioned above, the only way to learn and change the physical experience is to work through it firsthand. For example, all humans will know suffering and eliminate suffering after they have experienced it firsthand. After we experience something and heal it, we use the lesson in our evolution. We can learn from our first-hand experience not to be the cause of others' suffering because we experienced a life and time, or perhaps many lives, in which we ourselves have suffered. Another example is a void of love. We may have had multiple lives in which we took love for granted and didn't appreciate our loved ones as we should. To heal and repair this, we might make a soul level decision to deprive ourselves of love so that we can learn to appreciate its value.

"One needed loneliness so that one may fully understand and appreciate love to its fullest potential - in all of its glory and perfection. Every drop worth the wait. A thirst made stronger as it was carried through many lives. You now enjoy every quenching of that thirst so much more than the rest of the population. You now find, see and feel appreciation in every drop of love's presence, in every aspect of love's being with so much more appreciation than before."

-Jessenia Nozzolillo

Just like building muscle, we cannot build it up without first ripping the muscle apart. We learned appreciation through experiencing a void. We learned the beauty of love, through a lack of it. We cannot truly understand an emotion until we experience it and its opposite first hand and full-force in this physical world. Sometimes those experiences bring beauty, sometimes they bring pain. The power is in releasing the pain. Holding onto the anger or pain of your past will not hurt the person who hurt you. They move on with their life. Because everything is energy; reliving the pain in your mind daily and remembering them daily is feeding them energy. This energy exchange means they are still connected to you and still able to leech off your energy. The best way to cut them off and to close the pain is to release the situation all together. Do not block the situation, release it. Continuously, the best way to break and release pain is to find the lesson or beauty in that experience. At soul level, we see and understand the larger picture of the plan. I myself was a victim of rape, I would never wish that on anyone. But I had no barriers, no self-esteem, no self-worth. I was covered in layer after layer of oppressive negative thought forms and shells. Every negative experience I had experienced created a shell and I was still trapped in the shell of my experiences. Now I know that rape was a response to my energy. I was carrying so much pain I called pain to me. I called the person forward blinded to all the other ways they were horrible for me and to me. I put myself in a comprisable situation because I didn't respect myself and truly didn't care for my safety. This is an extreme example of this negative shell response and it's important to understand all situations are unique. I was so out of balance, even creating relationships with my rapist because I didn't understand what was happening or how to protect myself. That is a lesson I will never take for granted. In this lesson I have learned that I am a beautiful sensual woman, worth respecting. I learned respect of women and their bodies. I learned energetic intrusion and how to respect not only physical boundaries, but energetic boundaries. I released the pain and found healing in myself. I released their connection to me and found beauty in my curves, love in my touch and power in my step because my body will now always be mine and mine only to explore, love and control. My relationship with my body and sexuality was not harmed, because I healed and learned, as opposed to dwelling and suffering. I didn't want to give my abuser that kind of power over me, so I took back my power. Every time I reverted to the place of pain and suffering, I reminded myself that Bob Marley was a product of rape. In his lifetime, he helped millions see their own worth. Our mothers' stories, courage, and hope gave me hope to keep looking for the light in my own pain. Their experience guided me into courage and healing.

Have you ever accomplished anything from clinging to vengeance, dwelling, suffering, or reliving trauma? No. No one ever has! But you will accomplish anything you desire when you learn to let the pain transmute into beauty and growth. And no, it's not hard. Speaking as a survivor myself, it's much harder to sit in that pain your whole life, reliving the trauma. It's much more painful to refuse healing and growth and continue to fester in your wounds. IT IS SO HARD, to see your pain manifest and relive in your children! Because when we don't heal, the pain continues. It is much easier to allow healing and allow change. It is significantly easier to change the cycles and walk free from the chains that weigh you down. The issue is that humans are terrified of change. They are terrified of change more than they are fearful of pain. They become comfortable and familiar with the pain. They allow the pain to live in their daily existence and become accepting of it. They also believe that trauma defines them. Trauma doesn't define you, it molds you but only when you have released that trauma can you see the masterpiece created in the process of your growth. For a second think, what would the world look like if we removed all pain, heartache, and sadness from art? Art in many ways is what pain CAN BE when healed. Just the same, has negative self-talk ever served you? Has it ever made you feel better? Was it ever the reason you were able to get out of bed and accomplish anything? No. If it's clearly not working, try something new. How about encouraging yourself? How about speaking to yourself with kindness and love? How about supporting yourself? You will get completely different results when you change the behaviors and thought patterns inhibiting your growth. You will get completely different results when *you* stop getting in the way of your growth.

Change your thinking from, "You are a loser and will never get anything right" to, "That's amazing for your first try, imagine what you can accomplish the second time around?"

The voice and role you play in your own development sets the stage for who you become.

I truly understand firsthand the pain and trauma that comes from a life of abuse, violence, sexual abuse, poverty, homelessness, loving addicts, suffering pedophilia and rape. I am in no way trying to be insensitive to anyone's personal experiences. I am simply sharing the system of healing that was channeled to me and assisted in my own development and healing. I also understand and truly believe that there is no growth in victim mentality. I now understand, and truly believe that you must shift out of that mentality and into "divine creator of your reality" mentality to find the healing necessary to grasp and overcome that which blocks us.

So, as you move forward please remember that just because something bad happened to you does not mean something bad has to *keep* happening to you. Just because you experienced trauma does not mean trauma has to *keep* following you. Just because you've been stabbed by a knife doesn't mean you have to *keep* picking up the knife and stabbing yourself. Bad circumstances do not become bad lives. They can and will if you allow them, but that is a choice you make every day. This is so important because in taking blame out of our experiences, we are left with confronting ourselves, our emotions and our rebuilding process. It truly doesn't matter who did what to you, what matters is how you choose to respond and rebuild yourself after the trauma has occurred. Every life has the ability to be your greatest masterpiece, what will you create with the material you were given?

A block that inhibits our current life may have originated in this life or a past life. That is something I would see in a personal reading. This is important to understand because many times we don't even realize there is a block. We simply know we aren't progressing or materializing new things and positive change and aren't sure why. This is because we were born with this block so it's very much a part of who we are in our current lives. Therefore, understanding it and breaking it down is that much more necessary (there is more of this in the section on past lives). For example, here is a story of a block that manifested in a past life.

This is a story about a Victorian-era woman. She never had to struggle financially or go without anything growing up. When she was old enough she was married off by her father to another family for political gain and to strengthen the family name.

In this time, women had few rights, and many were entirely dependent on fathers and husbands for support and care. This left her feeling like a victim of money. If she had been poor, no one would have really cared who she married. She might have had some choice in the matter or at least more options. This is a classic "grass is greener" perspective. She even wished to be poor because she thought if she was poor it would be easier for her to revolt and have more freedom. Even though her husband was handsome, every night she was forced to have sex with him and it felt like rape from a stranger. She had no say. It was her "duty". After it was done, he was off to work. They barely knew each other and barely ever got to know each other as he was very busy with politics and work.

The only solace she found in this life was when she finally had a child and that child brought her happiness. Even then, she had no rights to the child. She was told how to raise him and what kind of mother she should be. In the desperation of that life she promised herself she never wanted money again as it meant she had to sacrifice who she was and what she wanted. She brought that trauma forward and believed she would never be able to have both money and happiness because in that past life it was true. Removing this block and healing this past life, she was able to change blocks to having both in this life and change the repeated pattern that had haunted her in this life.

Judgment is another common block I find and a trigger for a necessary lesson. If you are experiencing judgment toward someone, it is because you have places in yourself to heal. What triggers you is a direct reflection of places within that need healing.

An example, I was at the store and a lady stopped to look at children's books. I thought, "Wow, look at that woman so concerned about her children's education. Buying books. Good for her." Then I realized I didn't look at books. In no way did that mean I wasn't concerned about my children's education. In fact, I didn't stop because I have so many books that I just didn't need anymore. We had just taken boxes of books out to donate the day before. But in an instant, I had assumed that everyone who wasn't shopping for books must not care about their children's education simply because of my own temporary limited thought patterns at the time. At that very instant - I was projecting taught thought patterns and limitations out onto my environment in the form of judgment.

In another scenario, an older woman in line was shuffling through her bag counting pennies. I was irritated. I was in a rush. My life is always go, go, go. I didn't want to wait any longer. She turned to me and apologized. I then stopped to analyze my body language and energy and responded "No, don't be sorry. You have every right to take your time." I understood that I was unintentionally reflecting and projecting my busy life and deadlines on others when really that's my own scheduling issue. I was aggravated that I crammed my day with obligations, not aggravated that someone else needed time to pay.

Another great and common example is that I judged others on the way they dressed. I assumed women who showed skin were promiscuous and "trashy". I realize now that I was simply acting and reacting from a place of sexual trauma. My body was never protected and my self-esteem highly damaged, so I was expressing my own pain in never feeling comfortable in my own skin and never feeling safe to wear what I wanted. My insecurities and fears were projecting outwards onto others in the form of judgment.

Why is self-love and healthy self-esteem important? Because the insecurities we hide, are judgment. Every criticism you allow from yourself is a criticism you allow, enforce, and project onto others.

Therefore, one who criticizes self - cannot find healing because they are still criticizing the population. For example, if you feel you are being ranked, it's because you still believe in a ranking system. You still believe some people are better than others. MOST of that time, the victim of your ranking system it you! You believe you are unworthy or lower on some totem you created in your mind. If we are still criticizing self, we will then reflect those standards and criticisms onto the population. Meaning we are still in a place of judgment also meaning we are inhibiting the growth of the collective conscious through judgment.

That is where the connection between wisdom and simplicity come into play. This is also part of the never-ending cycle in which we trap ourselves. All labeling is a limitation we set on ourselves and others, from mathematical to scientific concepts. As our labels grow so does the feeling of separation the labels and categories create. Labels are necessary for processing information into the physical mind, but they are not necessary in the soul which interprets energy not labels. Labels create systems, layers, pillars, placements, value, standards. So, it is true that in our obsession with labeling and categorizing we have truly separated our souls from our other bodies and have gone so far out of balance that we even began to limit and manage our own abilities into these very small limited, categorized microsystems of measurement and labels. In truth though, we are magnificent, limitless, expansive energetic fields. We are liberated and immense in every way. So don't mix the way your physical mind stores information to the way your subconscious mind stores information.

After we shed our obstructions and blocks to our energetic bodies it becomes easier to see and understand these triggers are call to immediate growth. I no longer let these judgment and labeling triggers dwell. I address them immediately knowing that they will just keep popping up and inhibiting me if I don't. I even have fun looking for the hidden lesson, knowing I am in the process of unlocking another soul truth.

Although we spend plenty of time obsessing over every single detail during the soul-planning process, our plan doesn't always go as we hoped. Nevertheless, we still have free-will. This means that somebody can come down to Earth and ditch the map, just choosing to live a different life way off the paved roads and pre-thought paths created in the Akashic Realm. Because of this, we don't create all our realities at once. Our level one weavers (one of the many soul-level jobs) wait until we make decisions to create or weave the reality of that decision. They begin to weave in the people, places, situations necessary to make that decision a reality. We then have a level up on the weavers. Level 2 weavers are the program creators. They drop on the larger programs necessary to create the reality attached to your decisions. It's like a boost to manifesting. Behind these workers we have the "matrix workers" or level 3 weavers and they are the ones that put the program together in whole; our whole physical reality. Global events, weather etc. This whole process is created to make our reality on Earth a learning experience. Everything is experience. We must physically experience everything to learn new things in this physical world.

I once asked God why he allows his children to suffer if he loved us and he said this to me, "You love your child. He is everything to you. And still you sign him up for football knowing that there is a possibility he can get hurt, or even die. You sit on the sidelines, biting your nails, praying and hoping he won't get hit, hurt, even killed. But he wanted this. He wanted the experience. He wanted to be part of a team. Be part of something greater. He wanted the experience and the physical development and knowledge that came with the experience, so you allowed him to have the experience. You even signed off on the papers knowing the risks involved. You know you can't run out on to the field every time he gets hurt. You know you can't keep him from the experience and growth. And with all experience comes the possibility of harm. It's the same. You wrote this life. You chose this experience. You begged me for it. You wanted to learn and expand your understanding of your physical world. I had no choice but to support your thirst for growth, even if it meant you might suffer in the process. It doesn't mean I love you less. If anything, I love you enough to support your decisions and growth regardless of fear. Uninhibited by my needs. Unconditional love."

Chapter 6

Spiritual Gifts And Their Blocks

———∿∽◦⌒⊙⌒◦∽∿———

"We are all gifted. We all have deeply embedded soul gifts that I can see. We have all experienced pain. We have all experienced loss. We have all experienced heartache. If you have been lucky enough to avoid it in this life, I guarantee it's happened in a past life. So, what is the difference with how we perceive the world if we are all truly created equal?

Simply put: what separates you is your ability to transmute pain into experience without letting it weigh you down. Your ability to keep standing and rebuilding. Your ability to walk through the fire and come out a more beautiful, divine creation. A warrior. A messenger of light, love and healing."

—Jessenia Nozzolillo

So many times, it's those who seem to have it put together that need the most healing. You see, those who some might consider "basket cases", those who are emotional and spill everything have already begun the journey of healing. They have already begun ripping apart the stories that ail them. They have already begun the reconstruction process. Those that seem "normal" many times are the ones having a hard time dealing with or even acknowledging their blocks. Many times, they are also the ones that deny the concepts we are discussing even exist! They simply aren't ready to begin the process of healing and face themselves in that manner. Those cases can be the hardest. You must start from scratch. They have invested so heavily on their current structure and often have no interest in rebuilding. So many times, it's the gifted sensitives that have taken on the hardest lives. They take on many traumatizing experiences so that they may learn to heal those kinds of experiences in others and the world.

How many times have you said to yourself: "I'm at the mercy of others' emotions?" or "Being too sensitive is a weakness", "I can't leave my house", "I'm on an emotional rollercoaster", "Absorbing the energy, pain and emotions of those around me is exhausting", "Being a source of energy for energy vampires is ruining me."

If this sound familiar to you, understand something that took me 30 years to figure out on my own: your energy is yours to control, give, use. *Stop* giving it away! That is an active choice you are making to be so influenced by others.

These are simply the symptoms of undeveloped gifted souls with many different gifts and abilities. Stop being the victim of your gifts and develop them! When I investigate the energetic body for gifts, I see them filed in different chakras (see Chakra Gift Chart). I see gifts play out very differently depending on the soul. Sometimes I see one major gift and other smaller supporting gifts. Sometimes I see many small gifts that work together to create one large gift. Sometimes I see multiple major gifts and minor supporting roles. Sometimes we have guides that work specific chakras and gifts. This means that your gift is large and in need of immediate development. In this scenario, your guide would be a direct teacher in developing that gift in this current time. We would work to establish our connection to that guide and allow them to do their job, guiding us into developing the gift. We also have future life gifts, this means we have gifts that are not intended to open until we have lived lives written and played out in our future selves. As we open our gifts, use them and practice, you will see your gifts develop and even evolve. A gift for reading animals' emotions might evolve into a gift of reading human energy. This might evolve to reading universal energy. If a gift has evolved in strength you may awaken a guide for the gift that is now reaching a stage that needs guidance from a higher source. The guide comes through to help guide you in evolving that gift to its full potential. I have not seen whole gift systems that are like others. I have seen gifts that repeat in others, but usually the remainder of their gifts are different and unique to them depending on where they are developmentally.

Many times, we improperly use these gifts. This improper use comes from our difficulty in really understanding the gift. If we have a gift to pick up the emotions of others, this can be helpful in helping them heal and connecting with them. Then we might also possess another gift that allows us to process and flush out energy that isn't ours. Not being aware of the system and how it goes together, would be like taking a bath and then not knowing that we can also drain the dirty water before we use the tub again. The emotional energy will accumulate and cause physical, emotional, and mental blocks and ailments until we feel paralyzed by the filth making ourselves sick.

Gifts are woven into the soul at the time of the soul's creation and they are unlocked when we have encountered the experience and trigger for releasing the gift. After the gift has opened we explore its possibilities. Sometimes that means we must explore lives in which we were affected by ego, thirst for power, greed and used the gifts inappropriately. But, I truly believe that those lives are necessary in discovering our full potential and removing ego and thirst for power. Again, we cannot understand the darkness of greed without experiencing it first-hand in one of our lives. If you use your gifts for assistance and "good" in this life it is because you have already learned that lesson first-hand in a past life. I have yet to come into a situation where a gift was taken from a soul without permission. The only time I came close to this is when someone didn't know about their gifts and thus used them incorrectly because they didn't understand or know what was going on. It became so bad that the person suffered an overdose and almost lost their life. As we have explored earlier, some people seek out and unfortunately abuse drugs to numb their own gifts. At this point, higher-self and council agreed to shut off gifts in this life so that the person would no longer risk her life.

Although judgment is not necessary, and we have reviewed judgment in many forms throughout this book, Source will never energetically fund a gift used for negativity or harm. In these circumstances, that is people sometimes resort to other gods, deities and goddesses. One may also resort to syphoning their personal energetic body, taking from physical appearance, health or from syphoning the environment or nature. This is what we would refer to as **leeches** or **energy vampires** and workers of the **dark magic**, **voodoo**, and so forth. Animal sacrifice is one of these forms of energy transference or syphoning. They are transferring the life of an animal to fund work that will not be funded by Source. And again, no judgment needed. They are experiencing their life and lessons as needed and as we have once experienced before in a previous (or even current) life! But always keep in mind, you must replace what you take, whether that be in this life or then next, Karma needs to be paid. I myself have had lives in which I had to learn to release greed and ego, but I can say confidently having experienced both that there is no power in separation. In causing harm to anyone, you are funding the idea of separation. In causing harm to one, you are funding the idea that we are not all connected and all on the same path. You are disconnecting yourself from the collective, thus minimizing your own power. So, although people may feel like they are more powerful this way because of the temporary jolt or adrenaline functions quickly on the physical plane, it truly and very simply isn't so. True power comes with accepting you are one of the collective, with reconnecting to soul, with finding healing and through love. As Source represents unconditional love to all its creations, we disconnect ourselves from the whole when we do anything against that love. If you want to be powerful, tap into the collective self and universal love.

Usually, the gifts I read and pick up are gifts that need to be worked on in this life and gifts that have the ability to open in this life even further. Sometimes these gifts have past life or current life obstructions and those would also come up. Sometimes I see future life gifts *if* the person needs to begin the process of establishing those gifts in this life and *if* the information is necessary and useful for this current life.

Guilt can block our gifts. Although we are not punished for how we use our gifts here on earth, we may feel tremendous guilt for things we have done on earth after reverting to soul self. If our gifts were involved in those actions we regret, we may remove or punish ourselves for the way we used our gifts.

As I've discussed, I have had my gifts throughout my entire life. I have also possessed them in other lives as well. In other lives I, was persecuted, held captive, and used against my will so that others could benefit from my skills. In some of my lives I was well respected and taken care of. The violent lives scared me from "coming out" in this life and reliving the pain of being abused and used.

Even though I was aware of my huge mission in this present life, I really wasn't ready to "step into the light" or "come out of the closet" until my mid to late-20s. The fear and trauma of those lives lingered. But my gifts started getting more and more powerful until I didn't really have a choice *except* to use them and release that energy.

Did I lose people in my life? Yes, I did. There are people that I thought would always be there for me and support me but instead have been pulling away from me. That's okay! As you shed your limitations and boundaries, people participating in those limitations and boundaries will naturally fade. Since the beginning of time, people have feared what they don't understand. I know better than to take it personally now, although that wasn't always the case. Now I teach understanding in order to reduce the fear and misconceptions that put me and many other gifted souls in danger for so many lifetimes.

In shedding the old I have made space for the new. I have met an amazing new group of spiritual people who have overcome tremendous obstacles and have huge hearts ready to take on the world and reestablish balance, love and light.

As for permission for energetic readings, everyone has different perspectives on this. I believe that if you try to "pick up" someone's soul over a distance *without* their permission you are only going to see what you want to see. I also know that our higher-selves give us permission sometimes even when our physical bodies and minds are not aware that we gave that consent. For example, if you are a child. You as a child don't know you need help, but your parent might seek help on your behalf. Therefore, your soul, being all knowing, might allow access for the assistance even if the child was too young to be aware or unable to verbally consent to help. Many times, your soul is that parent, seeking help on your behalf, understanding more then we do and more than we can physically comprehend. I also know that most humans don't understand their energy or souls and walk around like open books hoping for someone to touch the pages and understand them, help them, and guide them.

I truly believe that reading people without their physical permission is useless. By reading without permission, you are only making observations about people they don't want to hear. If they wanted to hear it - they would ask. It's a waste of your time to be invading someone's space or privacy without their permission and it's a waste of time for the person that you're bothering because they simply aren't ready if they didn't ask for the unwanted "advice".

It is also important to understand that our souls and bodies are incredibly different. If you are reading someone's soul then you're likely going to see the beautiful, all-knowing, loving, healing energy and wisdom that souls are. If you pay attention to the physical body or person, it's a whole different story. Our souls and bodies are different. So "judging" or making decisions on who someone is at soul level is a dangerous thing to do, as humans don't always have the same intentions as their souls. This is one of the things that sets "sensitives" up for a lot of heartache.

Lastly, if I went around "open and receptive" to everyone's energy all the time I would have a nervous breakdown or suffer panic attacks. It is way too much for the human mind to digest at once. Self-control is self-mastery and it is necessary for strengthening gifts. I simply see too much to be open to everyone at the same time. Because one soul can have experienced hundreds of lives, there is a lot to feel, see, and explore. This doesn't include soul family, soul creation or origins, ailments, guides, gifts, and missions. So, control is necessary. Focus is necessary. Our gifts are not a punishment, but they may feel like it when we don't understand them and use them appropriately. So, I do not read people without their permission for millions of reasons, but these are my main ones and I hope you will follow the same guidelines.

We have discussed that blocked or misused gifts can manifest into physical ailments. In my readings, I have found gifted souls that inappropriately use their gifts ultimately manifest anxiety, eating disorders, depression, and many other ailments. I am not a doctor and cannot diagnose health problems. I do recommend people get medical help when experiencing these deep energetic ailments because they do become so thick and difficult that they need professional medical advice and sometimes even medication.

In using your intuition, you will need to build confidence. Intuition is 100% about shutting off the little voice inside that says "You are wrong, maybe it's not accurate. Maybe you'll offend them." Even if you never choose to read people professionally it is imperative to practice your intuition and skills on others. Practicing gives us the confidence we need to understand and trust our own intuition about our own lives in the future. Practice will strengthen your own ability to connect to higher-self and your abilities to analyze and release your own blocks. In reading others, we also get the ability to experience places of ourselves we didn't know were broken or needed healing. Incarnation on earth is a lot like college. We all take on courses, or in this case lives, for specific credits and to get specific knowledge and training. This means that we may have missions and lives like someone else's. We may have taken on similar lives and overcome similar lessons. By assisting others, you do heal issues within yourself, even if you don't know where those places are and in which life they took place. This is like getting a head-start on healing and removing blocks *before* they slap you in the face! It is a beautiful thing!

Next let's examine the practice of grounding. Grounding is vital! I mentioned this before and it is worth mentioning again. We are not sources of energy, we are conductors of energy. Considering this, it is very important we ground our energy properly. When we heal, read, access higher-self, or meditate, we are using a combination of energy from source as well as earth. Earth's connection is what we consider grounding. Many people don't understand or know the value in Earth's connection. When we are properly grounded we are strong, stable, clear, and most importantly properly flushing any negative emotions and energy back to Earth for energetic recycling. Earth is perfectly adapted and able to remove negativity form your energetic body and recycle the energy. When we are unproperly grounded, our energy will drain quickly, we may feel unfocused or like a kite with no anchor. Improper grounding will also very quickly drain us when we are in public or reading others unintentionally - because we will end up using our own energy without a proper root connection or anchor. Grounding is a visual process of attaching the root chakra to earth, like an anchor is a part of the guided meditation in the beginning of the book. Just like any other skill, the more you ground your energy the easier it will be.

After you release your blocks and obstructions you will become very familiar with your new energetic body. When all these blockages are removed it is easier to feel and see when someone else wants to intrude into your energy and unload their garbage onto you. You will immediately sense and return the garbage or release it to Earth. Until that process becomes routine and natural for you, here is the system I used:

I scan my body in the morning before going out, very aware of what I have and don't have in my energy. Then I can consciously be aware of any new pains and emotions that try entering my experience and shoo them off before they have the chance to create any issues. I then re-scan and release everything at the door before entering my house. I never want to bring the energy I picked up outside of my home into the home I worked so hard to charge with positive energy and healing because what you bring home will then attach and linger around your loved ones. I also do another scan in the shower where I imagine everything I don't need being washed off by the rushes of water as it nourishes and replenishes my energy. Water is a great conductor of energy and when I was first opening to my abilities, a lot of startling things would happen while I was in the shower. Voices, messages, visions would all come to me and they would be very vivid. Now this happens to me all the time, but it's much easier for me to manage. I no longer need to worry about getting bombarded by my guides while naked and vulnerable. The same things may very well happen to you as you begin to open and learn to use your gifts.

Setting energetic barriers in public is another important skill to understand as you develop and become stronger. This will help protect your energy in the meantime. To do this, I envision one-sided reflective opalite pyramid over my body that moves with me when I'm in busy or high-energy places. This helps keep me focused and keep my energy where I need it. Through the top of the pyramid I can still access Source energy and through the bottom I stay grounded. The shape itself a reminder of the importance of grounding. Everyone will eventually come up with their own ideas and systems that work best for them. Once you read your charts and begin to learn how to use any gifts you have, your process for grounding will develop. Additionally, trauma in all lives is usually found in the root chakra. The root chakra is the place where our survival instincts lie. Remember that if you have a hard time grounding and have had a difficult present or past life. It's a reminder that we still haven't worked through our past and current life trauma. Releasing that trauma is imperative to strengthen your grounding system and to help you establish a stronger connection.

Being able to *not* pick up on others personal thoughts and energetic debris is also another imperative skill for those developing their gifts. Usually we connect and read others person to person. Most readers read this way. And when they do they are essentially picking up everyone's energetic debris. We as humans carry a lot of trash and debris in our energy! We have discussed many versions of this negative type of energy and they include jealousy, anger, fear, stress, judgments, and criticism. When you don't understand energy and are reading on the physical plane, this can feel very heavy and dark. Understand that even this is a lesson. If you are feeling an "attack" or judgment, it is a reflection of that person's insecurities and thoughts and not your own. Again, with judgment, sensitives may also be sensitive to the thoughts of others (if that is one of your gifts). Always note that reading people on the physical plane will pick up a lot of "thought junk" you will hear all their insecurities projected in judgment, or aggression. You might hear their boring mental busy talk. You may hear them scanning over your body and appearance. Always keep in mind that anything you hear at this level is a direct reflection of them not you. For example, hearing "Who does she think she is dressing like that." Should and will eventually translate to "I sense you have issues embracing your sexuality and body."

At soul level with enough practice and experience. If you are not careful with how you pick up and interpret this energy, It might accumulate becoming too thick to interpret or be too heavy on your own energetic body. When we used the guided meditation at the beginning of the book, we learned to open to higher-self and let higher-self pick up and interpret the readings. That is where we find growth. That is where we find the beautiful unbiased information we need to help further healing. That is the energetic bridge we want and need to strengthen. It's a great system to protect your own energy from this heavy energetic debris and intrusion.

Many people come to me with the fear their own energy has been intruded upon or that they are being manipulated. This can happen, and quite frequently. We are very influenced by the people who surround us as energy will mix. When you know and understand your energy and your gifts, you simply have an easier time not allowing this to happen. You are accessing the highest vibrational energy available to you and the only people who can penetrate that energy are people at a higher level. In perfect "coincidence", those who have raised their own vibration know energetic intrusion is not a respectful use of their own gifts. So essentially, people can only access, manipulate and disrupt your energy if you allow it. Whether it be through ignorance or desperation, or poor energetic boundaries, you must allow it somehow at some level. As I mentioned earlier, some people walk around like open books because they are desperately seeking healing from anyone who may understand them. This would be a great example in letting your energy be intruded upon by everyone around you. If you are walking around like an open book hoping someone will touch your pages and give you an answer to your sadness, then your pages will get dirty. Answers are found within. Thus, the whole purpose of my system: helping you find the connection you need to listen to your own intuition. In the end, everyone's opinion of you is nothing and the only thing that matters is how you see yourself. By accepting people into your life, you also accept their energy. Remember that when letting those toxic relationships linger.

This three-report system and class is exactly what you need to understand and unlock your soul to its full potential. With this information you will be drawn to what makes your soul truly happy. You will reconnect to your purpose and path and soul. This gives us a clear path and direction into why we incarnated and what we need to continue moving forward. Staying true to this path and plan truly brings us abundance and happiness.

Chapter 7

Tools Of Divination And Using Your New-Found Intuition

———⁓⁓◦◖◦◗◦◖◦◗◦◖◦⁓⁓———

We all have soul gifts deeply woven into out energetic structure. As we evolve, learn, and develop self-control, our gifts begin to open. Sometimes some gifts are not available in this life because we have simply not reached the place and time in which they become available. In that case, tools of divination are always available to you and a great way of connecting to your higher-self. All tools of divination are simply an extension of your soul or higher-self. The purpose of a tool of divination is to give you a physical cue to what you are hearing, seeing, and sensing in spirit or energy. We, especially in the beginning of our practice and work, will question ourselves repeatedly. Learning to use a tool of divination will help you focus and explore your own energy work through your doubt with a visual representation of your higher-self.

Many people have intense systems for reading and connecting to their tools of divination. I personally do not. I feel and know that our tools are simply an extension of our higher-self. Because of this, I regard my higher-self as my strongest tool. I feel like we project a lot of our doubt, biases, beliefs and learned behavior onto our tools. For example, someone may say, "I didn't sleep with my cards under my pillow last night, so they are mad and won't give me the information I need." Your cards are a projection of your own energy. You are fearful of the truth and thus blind to it. You were likely not willing to take in the answer, or you went into the reading with doubt, thus projecting doubt in the answer. Simply put, it is you not giving yourself the information you need. Some people also say you must be gifted a deck of Tarot cards. I don't agree with this at all. I feel like picking a deck you love and are drawn to is where we find that deep connection to our tools of divination. Additionally, many people will read for themselves and completely skip all the negative aspects of the card or tool - only seeing the positive. In removing the negative, we can't obtain the positive. Remember, never to skip the negative. It is an important and necessary part of making the reading as accurate as possible and many times is the answer to how you will be getting the positive. When I read tarot or oracle cards for myself, I will say, "use the book definition for this answer", and I will pull the card and read the book. I do this because I understand I am biased to my own energy and if it is written in the book word-for-word it becomes harder to ignore. Usually decks come with a book. If you don't have a book find a website that resonates with you. I love biddytarot.com.

It is also important to set a tone and intention with your tools. Set rules that will stay engrained throughout your lifetime. For example, in the case of using a pendulum for dowsing, you would need to know that a counter clock wise swing means no. There is no questioning that. Setting clear boundaries makes your readings clear. Always set very direct and clear intention and ask very clear, specific questions. Simply asking, "will things get better" is careless phrasing that presents a lot of interpretations. How your pendulum swings will be unique to you. Make sure to establish your own YES, NO, or MORE INFORMATION and understand that will stay the same through your lifetime.

When preparing to read or use a divination tool, it is necessary to properly open your energy. You can reference the guided meditation. There is no such things as a bad or evil tool. Tarot cards, Ouija boards, and scrying mirrors are not dangerous. A tool is always neutral. The risk comes from the reader who is not properly grounded or open. If one is not open to the proper dimension before using tools of divination, one may channel lower level energies. This is important to understand and implement as part of your routine. Once you've established a strong energetic bridge for connecting, it will become a faster process. This means you must also make it a habit to close or bring in your energy after a reading, psychic connection or meditation so that you can function and focus properly with the conscious mind as to not drain yourself.

The tools you are drawn to will depend where your gifts lie and who your guides are. If you have Angelic guides they will likely be drawn to crystals, Angel cards, Oracle cards, bells and chimes. If you have Earthly gifts, they may draw you to candles, crystals, herbs or oils. Know that not every tool will resonate with your energy but stick to the ones that do resonate with you and your gifts.

After you learn what your gifts are, it's easier to find tools and methods that compliment your gifs and their locations in the chakras. Choosing a tool that compliments your energy is important as, again, their functions are extensions of your own energy. The following is a list of popular divinatory tools as well as other useful implements for you to incorporate into your practice.

Pendulum—A pendulum is anything on a cord, chain or rope that can swing back and forth. It has a weight at the bottom, usually with a point. In times of crisis, I even used my wedding ring threaded with a piece of hair. The pendulum will swing clockwise for yes or no and counter clockwise for the other. Always establish this before a reading and know that it will be the same every time thereafter. A pendulum that doesn't move is telling you that the question is too vague or indirect or that it may have not been decided yet. You can only read futures and decisions that have been decided. Some people will develop a routine by asking questions like, "Is it true and accurate that..." whatever it is that resonates with you is appropriate. Just remember that a pendulum or any other tool is not enchanted with magic, it works as an extension of your own abilities and higher-self. Even for practitioners of magic, though they may use tools of divination as part of magical practice, *they* are the ones with the gifts and the tools are an extension of that. Unless, of course, they have intentionally enchanted or energetically altered the tool.

Symbols—Some people see symbols and therefore can utilize them as a form of divination. Depending on your gift structure, these symbols are a quick way to deliver vast amounts of information. People with gifts in the 3rd eye may resonate and see many symbols. Placement of the symbol in important. Where is it in relation to the body? Pins by the feet can represent foot pain, problems walking or moving forward. Pins by the head would represent a whole different issue. Color of the symbol in important to understand and likely connects to the chakras. What feeling came with the symbol? Sadness? Fear? Anxiety? Is the symbol representative of an animal, shape, color, word, constellation? They are all relevant! You may see the symbol of a chakra or a Wiccan symbol or sigil. Stick to your strengths. If you are seeing a lot of sigils, then get to know and understand them. If you are seeing a lot of animals, get to know and understand the energies you get when seeing the animal. The ability to see and interpret symbols can provide us a lot of information in our day-to-day, but it can also be a difficult gift to master. The best and fastest way to do this is to keep a key. Understand that blue is always going to represent the same thing. That a cross will always represent the same thing and keep a key for your own reference as you figure this out. Also understand that your symbols are speaking to you, not anyone else. What does this mean to *you*? How do *you* interpret the information being brought forward? Your higher-self will always speak a language you understand. Your key will become your own personal language between you and your guides.

Dreams—Dreams are always relevant. If we are highly stressed in our environment we will have stressful dreams or nightmares. Fear may present itself as paralysis. Dreams function on symbolism. I always recommend keeping a dream journal by your bed so that you can record your dreams. Look for the themes in the descriptions. Many times, when we descriptively write out the symbolism it begins to make sense to us and over time we will notice patterns. Also keep in mind that fear may visit us in a dream simply to get us to remember something. Fear creates adrenaline and that shocks our physical body into slightly awakening long enough to imprint or remember the message that follows. Ask yourself, is this fear a hint to pay attention to and remember what's next? We all also astral travel (reference astral travel below for more information). Some people confuse memories of astral travel with dreams.

Colors—Colors usually represent the chakras. I would stick to using the chakra chart, unless you are feeling they speak differently to you in your personal interpretations. Depending on your gift this could be so! Always trust what resonates with your own intuition.

Astral travel—We all also astral travel. It means that at night when we are asleep our soul will go pick up new information, join a class, work, visit family members, travel dimensions, attend spiritual events - whatever it is. Yes, we have classes and workshops on the soul level that we attend for evolution and to prepare us for upgrades. This is common. Understand that your higher-self knows what it's doing. Don't interfere, because you won't succeed. Have faith that your higher-self is always in control. They have done this since the beginning of humanity. It is normal. Some people have the gift of astral travel, which just means they can do this consciously and while awake.

Automated writing—This is an extension of channeling. It is simply taking in information and letting your higher-self guide your hand. It is a distraction of the conscious mind and allowance of the subconscious that moves our hand to direct messages and information. We distract the mind with a physical job, in this case holding a pen (also same with pendulum, cards etc) and allow the subconscious to direct our hand and write. This works best when people have a gift of channeling.

Channeling—Allowing higher level energies or beings to come through your throat chakra to deliver healing and loving messages. If we are not connected to higher-level energies or are under any inhibiting influence (drugs, alcohol) we may find we are channeling lower level energies and beings. This is dangerous for you and your loved ones.

Scrying—This is the process of seeing things and interpreting them. It is done by using a shiny, reflective, often black object like a mirror. Water, crystal balls, even fire are good for scrying. This is a great medium for people with third eye gifts. An ink blot test is a form of scrying. We see elements, symbols, and shapes in a surface that speaks to us at soul level representing the answers to what we are seeking. As you progress, you will simply see vivid video-like images - if this is one of your gifts.

Tarot cards—traditional tarot cards have colors, themes, and symbols displayed in intricate images or scenes on cards. They all mean something different, so it is important to examine each card and get to know them and learn how to interpret each one. Pay attention to the symbols that come forward and how they connect to the deck. I never use the instructional booklets that explain what each card is supposed to symbolize, because I truly believe my energy and higher-self will give me more intuitive information about the person than the book will. When I choose a card, I stare into the card and look for images, themes, words, feelings and put together the story they are telling me. Remember to stay focused and use intention when pulling a card so that your question is clear and directly connected to the cards that follow. Tarot usually has more specific meanings for card themes. Get familiar with the themes and understand that a Tarot deck has both "bad" and "good" meanings. Cards in reverse also have a meaning. When just beginning you may want to stick to only the upright definition. That's ok, if you establish that rule with your intuition, or higher-self beforehand. I feel that there is less "freedom of interpretation" in a tarot deck as they have a more universal theme than Oracle cards do. Tarot spreads have a meaning and flow. A **tarot spread** is the placement of a cards for an answer story. I myself have googled spreads online to look for a spread that would assist me in readings. You will see that certain spreads work best for certain answers.

Oracle cards—These are a lot like tarot cards in that they utilize colors, themes and symbols that all mean something. Pay attention to the symbols that come forward and how they connect to the deck. I never use the books (unless reading myself) because I truly believe my energy and higher-self will give me more intuitive information about the person than the book will. When I choose a card, I stare into the card and look for images, themes, words, feelings and put together the story they are telling me. Remember to stay focused and use intention when pulling a card so that your question is clear and directly connected to the cards that follow. Oracle cards can be any theme. They have funny cards, dragons, witch oracles, etc. There is more freedom of interpretation and it works best for the more visual reader as it requires more interpretation. Always look for the relation the person has to the card. For example, some people will simply read the card name, if it has one, and consider that a reading. I suggest looking at the theme between the cards drawn and asking, "How does this apply to this person specifically?"

Dowsing rods—These function very much like a pendulum. To use, one would hold the rods- one in each hand- and ask higher-self to establish a "yes" and a "no". Then ask the rods concise and clear questions. The rods respond by crossing each other or moving further apart.

Energetic healing—This is done by using energy, gifts or intuition to repair and flush disruptive energy in your clients or self, while filling and refueling the energetic body with energy from source. Everyone's energetic healing process will look very different depending on what your gifts are.

Animal totems—They are called many different things depending on cultural or spiritual background. In my personal connections, animal totems usually represent more temporary structures in someone's life. An animal totem can come in to represent a relationship between people, a current life situation, or a current block to growth. They can also come in for protection as "pets" to help us through certain aspects of our lives. I usually see spirit animals on the person and totem animals around the person. This would also depend on your belief system. I know there are people with gifts who function differently, and they may disagree. That is just how their higher-self speaks to them. I would look up totem animal definitions on google until you become familiar with each animal and its qualities. There are millions of animals- insects and mythical creatures included- that come through, not just the popular animals like wolves, owls, and deer. An example of a totem animal connection that came through during a reading was: a snake came in to represent shedding the old skin and habits to accept growth. This is not a spirit animal, but a totem used to represent a healing message or their temporary state of mind. All the terms and definitions in this book are definitions I have channeled myself in my own readings. I have a shaman guide who connects me to the animal aspects of my clients. There are millions of other definitions for what these represent and do change depending on the modality. The point is to establish a system that resonates with you and your gifts and to make sure you understand what each animal represents, to you! When I am reading my guides make it clear that a totem animal comes through as a temporary symbol. Spirit Animals come in as solid structures of the soul, regardless of our temporary events and obstacles. Soul animals don't change, totem animals may change from body to body or situation to situation. We would call on a totem animal for strength to overcome a situation, clarity or focus.

Spirit animals—usually a structural, solid part of someone's soul that doesn't change. One animal representing the physical body (in all lives), one representing the soul and another representing the mind (in all minds and incarnations) like a soul code. I find the animal representing the body by the feet of the person I am reading, the animal representing the mind by the forehead and the animal representing the spirit hovering right over their head. I would look up spirit animal definitions on google until you become familiar with each animal and its qualities. There are millions of animals (insects and mythical creatures) that come through so writing them all out is a whole other book!

Downloads and upgrades—These are pre-written in our astrological birth chart. They come in large energetic shifts and waves to help us shed old versions of ourselves and bring to light the new. This is where the sense of urgency comes to complete a shift or work on major change. The astrological cosmic soup would be fueling an upgrade that may pull you into a new career. That would be your window for the large shift. Some people ignore these, and change becomes harder after the cosmic soup has shifted and subsided. In many ways, it's easier to ride the waves and go with the flow. The flow is made to shift you.

Herbs, flowers, resins—All herbs and plants have an energetic signature that can be used to alter your energy and reality. Herbs are physical and work on a physical level. This means that the have an energetic, or magical property and a physical property. Basil can be burned to purify the air and bring in wealth or for wealth spells, or basil can be used in soup for flavor. Two different properties, same herb. Though burning herb bundles can assist in cleansing energy, air, houses and bodies, it does not remove negativity or lingering entities on its own.

Candles and wax readings—Similar to scrying, one would burn the candle with an intention and then read the leftover wax for messages, symbols and answers to the question.

Incense—Burned for its cleansing and purifying smoke, incense is made from flowers, herbs, and resins to create blends for various healing or spiritual purposes.

Potions—These are a combination of herbs, incense, essential oils, crystals, along with the energy of the maker. They are all specific to the creator and the creators gift system. Some clients with root chakra and sacral chakra gifts with earth may be drawn to using potions in their energy work.

Foods—Food can and should be used for healing! A clean, healthy diet can help clear your chakras and body. It can assist you unblock your third eye and continue to develop and elevate your gift. Many people use food like poison keeping us distracted and blocked while we "suffer" in the physical realm. Like everything else, food has a vibration. High vibrational foods like raw veggies, fruits, and nuts will assist you in elevating your energy. Many times, your soul will intuitively draw you to what the body needs. This is different then a craving. Although, if you are craving a lot of sweet foods after meditations, healings and connections it's likely because you aren't properly grounded.

Oils—Concentrated, distilled herbs and plants. Like herbs and plants, each oil has an energetic signature that can be used to alter your energy and reality. Like herbs, they are also physical with physical properties that can be different then their energetic properties and uses.

Bells, chimes, vibrational tuning, sound bowls—These tools work to correct the chakras in which they align to. Each chakra has a vibrational tone. These tools can be used to realign that vibrational tone - thus healing the chakra and loosening obstructions. This is a surface healing tool, not a deep energetic reconstruction tool.

Crystals—Crystals, stones, and minerals have healing vibrations. Each one is composed of different minerals and elements and therefore, each has a different healing or spiritual use and specialty. It is important that you give your crystals a job and charge them appropriately. In general, the color of the crystal will usually go with the chakra it assists. Crystals can be cleaned and recharged with selenite, cold water and salt, or a full moon. After buying a crystal, retune it by first cleansing it, then wearing it or carrying it close and giving it a job. How you clean and care for a crystal will depend on the crystal. Some don't do well with water, sunlight, salt, etc.

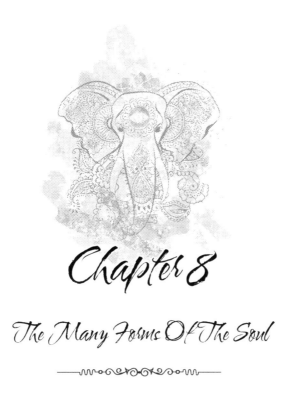

Chapter 8

The Many Forms Of The Soul

Souls, Hauntings and Orbs

This is one of the first questions I asked myself when I was discovering my own abilities. Why do souls appear to us in so many forms here on the physical realm? What's the difference between a haunting and an apparition? A haunting that repeats the same routine and one that intelligently responds to their environment? This will be something you might experience firsthand when connecting to higher-self.

Let's talk about this. When my mother and I were going on a "journey through our past" to release and heal old wounds, we traveled to many of the places we had lived. My mother suffered tremendous physical abuse at the hands of her exes. This one was a violent drug addict and drug dealer with a terrible temper. She was with him over 5 years and experienced a lot of pain at his hands. One incident in particular stands out. In this incident, he was choking my mother to the point where she died. She was blue and unresponsive. He panicked and resuscitated her. When she awoke and realized what happened, she panicked and jumped out the window of their second-floor apartment to the porch roof and climbed down and to the neighbors' door screaming for help and asking them to call the police. In this apartment, I was 1-3 years old. Too small to really remember anything. When we were looking for his apartment we parked at a playground. It had been 25 plus years since she had been to this neighborhood. She couldn't remember exactly where the apartment was. We stood in the center looking around trying to catch a memory or clue. The buildings had been painted, there was a new playground. Everything was different. Then all the sudden I could see the apparition of my mother jumping out of the second-floor window, in a white thin strapped nightgown, then run to the neighbor's door. I could see the haunting of my mother's trauma.

This was a mind-blowing experience for me. How could someone who is still alive, and right next to me create a haunting anywhere? It turns out that when we experience tremendous trauma and fear, a piece of our energy will stay in that fear, reliving the pain repeatedly until they are released. My mother's haunting had been reliving the same night, 20 times a day, for 25 years! This would surely leave an imprint on her own energy, obstructing healing, but left an imprint in that home. So, when we experience these traumatic events, it's important to check back with ourselves and release these current hauntings as they are a part of us and will continue to relive the pain if we allow them to.

These re-run hauntings are deeply embedded energetic programs. She "haunted" this place because that moment and time was fueled with so much fear, pain and desperation that it charged and remained in the area. This may also happen if someone has the same obsessive routine. They can leave a deeply embedded apparition in their home or environment of them repeating the same thing daily. Many times, they aren't "ghosts", they are instead soul fragments with deeply ingrained energetic patterns that have burned into that environment. They can communicate but usually only communicate information relevant to their imbedded memory.

Souls who have not crossed over are stuck between dimensions. A thin energetic **veil** separates our physical dimension from the soul dimension. They do overlap but are still separate. Soul dimension hovers slightly over our own. The veil can thin during certain astrological events and times of the year, and mediums have a gift of using a portal (like a door) to call in souls through the veil. They are always with us, right on the other side of that veil. The only time we see and feel them is when we call them over the veil (consciously or subconsciously), or when they are stuck here on earth. If they are stuck here on earth, they are usually considered a "haunting" and they are invisible to source energy, guides, and soul family. If they refuse to seek help, they cannot be helped. Many times, these souls are stuck because they are scared, looking for someone, confused about their death, or fearful of judgment and religious persecution when crossing over. They have very limited sources of energy and thrive in high energy currents here on earth. Just like the ocean, our world has **currents** of energy that are stronger than others and they get swept into these currents and use the local energy of the current to survive. Therefore, in a **haunted house**, or a house located on an energetic current, you will find souls that never physically lived in the house haunting it. They were swept up by the current and stay because they can use the energy from the area. You cannot get these souls to leave with sage. Burning sage is like spraying rotting food with perfume. It might smell better for a minute, but the source of the odor isn't gone. The only way to release these souls is if they release themselves or if they get counseled and convinced into crossing over. I call it ghost therapy. Many souls don't want to leave their home and are still waiting for a loved one they didn't realize already crossed over. Some are simply scared of judgment and others are waiting for forgiveness. A lot of children get stuck on this side because they simply don't know what happened to them and they are too scared to leave their parents' side. This can be heart-breaking, and therefore I don't like when people profit off hauntings by keeping the souls in that state of suffering. I feel that it is not right to profit off the pain of a soul. Some haunted houses will even make you sign waivers promising not to help the souls cross over.

Not all hauntings are simple souls who are stuck and need counseling. Some LOVE to scare people. Like I mentioned, the energy where they are stuck is very limited! They have very limited sources, so they like to take from our environment and energy. Fear is a great source of energy! The vamped-up adrenaline and fear gives them plenty of energy to feed off so that they can stay exactly where they are. Some souls are aggressively protecting a secret, reputation or item of value they obsessed over. In this case, they get very defensive and aggressive when you don't respect their boundaries. Some more reputable hauntings survive off the attention admiration of others. The fame keeps them alive.

There are also beings of other dimensions. These can be called upon and invited in to this dimension. This is so rare. You are more likely to get killed in real life than experience a dangerous being of another dimension. You are more likely to come across a dangerous human than a dangerous entity. They don't usually wander looking for chaos. Many times, they are invited in by people who simply don't understand what they are doing, or intentionally by people who believe they can control them. The negative dimensions of this side of the multiverse usually implode onto **the other side**. If the dimensions god, or creator, is negative; the goal of the soul group becomes negative and they lower their own vibration enough to implode. Once they implode through the barrier, they usually stay stuck unless a **being of the dark** can raise their vibration enough to escape the barrier. Raising your vibration is nearly impossible on the other side as it's simply not the goal. Chaos and disorder are the goal. Some wander through the boarders but it's important to understand they have no control over us unless we are also wandering the barrier. Sometimes we (at soul level) fight to move these dimensions ourselves as a protective measure and order of balance for our soul groups. The other side is much more dangerous for us as. These beings thrive in chaos and destruction. That is how they create and maintain energy. They very rarely escape to our side because their composition simply can't exist here for the most part.

Sometimes these dark energies and "monsters" can be created through intense thoughts and fears. If we fear something enough, that fear begins to create and materialize into an energetic being that will continue to feed off fear. Kids are usually the culprit for these. It's important to note they are created in the imagination, but with enough focus become "real". Energy starving the being by ignoring t is really the best way to remove it. In this situation, sage would work to clear the space.

Many times, people come to me feeling like they have a possession or attachment. They are usually not dangerous beings of lower dimensions, they are usually little gremlin-like energies that are created through vengeance, jealousy, anger. They are easy to remove and never anything too serious. Those who do find themselves with a lower level entity attachment or possession should seek professional help for removal. There are souls who specialize in that work and it is a part of their gifts. There are dimensions with different beings. Many of them aren't bad at all. But they do like to cause havoc when called in, and they do use us as a source of energy. Like wolves, wolves are not bad—but they are predators and don't like to follow human rules.

Souls who have crossed over are will present themselves in a healed, glowing manner. They may present themselves in the suit of their last incarnation or as higher-self. They usually stick to an appropriate, well presented form of themselves that will be recognized by the people they are coming through for. The only time a soul will show you their after-death form would be if they are still haunting.

Orbs are usually energetic workers coming in to do their job. They are a form of elementals (earth, wind, water, fire this also includes spirit or orbs). They might show themselves for support, guidance, to participate in an event or ceremony. Someone who has a gift of calling upon and guiding elementals can also call upon orbs. There are also elemental portals, which can be created, most of the time by accident. A **portal** is simply a door to another dimension. In this case a house, home, or location would have a lot of orbs or elementals. They can be mischievous, so this isn't always good. Elementals are what some people consider **fairies**. Many times, an orb is bringing a message or memory from a deceased loved one which is why they are so easily confused with ghosts. They are essentially **orbs** are spirit fairies or messengers.

Shadow people really get a bad rap. They are usually family members and deceased loved ones coming through and they simply don't have enough energy to fully appear because they would rather direct that energy toward communication. Some come in as a dense dark cloud that can scare us. But again, they are usually energies we know and hold dear. Never be afraid. But never invite anything in without knowing what you are doing. Shadow people are just a version of soul apparitions. A soul may come though as a fog, form, shadow or full-on apparition depending on how much energy they can derive from their environment. Most of the time, they don't because they would rather use the energy to send a message and communicate then spend it all on their appearance. It truly takes a lot out of them.

Guides can look like funny beings, they may take on weird shapes, sizes, and inhuman forms. They can come in as a full apparition or less dense energy.

When I see mediumship gifts in someone, I see a little portal above their head, like a crown. People have many gifts for this I call it the "Seers portal". They use this "door" to pull forward the being they wish to communicate with. Therefore, the guided meditation to properly opening and closing your energy is so important, because if you begin using this gift not knowing what you are doing, then you very well could let in a lower level energy or being that thrives off havoc. All souls are always available. If you grandmother crossed over and "isn't available" it is because the medium you are using cannot connect to her higher-soul. Her higher-soul is always available and can always come through as her. Sometimes they don't want to come through because they would rather be doing something else or because they aren't soul family. They might have played a role in this life that they are no longer connected to on the other side. The reason why your ex-husband's grandmother might come through is because she is soul family. She has soul connections to you. So as weird as it might be for you here on the physical level, it makes sense to her on the soul level. Some souls might shove their way forward in the connection because they have guilt about something, need to deliver a message or are seeking forgiveness. Sometimes they are just bored and want to chat, that's rare too. There is so much to do over there.

Which brings me to my next point, we have soul level jobs we take on. I myself am an akashic record guide and protector, at soul level, which is why I have access of the records. Some of us are healers, program creators, gatekeepers, life planners, child preppers, guides, travelers etc.!

In summary, never invite anything in unless you know what and who you are calling upon. The guided meditation in the beginning of the book will explain why and how to go about that in a safe and productive way. Never let a soul linger who doesn't want to cross over, somewhere someone is suffering without them by their side. Whether that be their higher-self, their soul-family, their soul group, or the other versions of themselves – they need to cross over and find healing. Never feed into the fear. Yes, haunted houses can be fun, and part of the process is getting scared. I'm talking about when you're experiencing something at home or anywhere else - understand fear is like candy to lower level energies and many times our fear is an invitation to stay and eat. By lower level energies, I mean they work and are made of low vibrational energies and that's why we associate them as "bad". When lower level energies cling to us, we cannot raise our vibration, we cannot continue our evolution, and we feel depleted. Many times, we also feel their negativity and weight.

Most healers and mediums can remove and repair these connections, depending on their gifts and their knowledge of their gifts.

Chapter 9

Past Life Journeying

"You cannot force consciousness. Consciousness can only be obtained when the individual chooses to seek it. What you can do is provide information, spread love and kindness to those who seek you. Just as your experiences shaped you, their experiences are still working to shape them and their perspectives into their own evolution. Be patient. Their time will come."

Jessenia Nozzolillo

I talked about this process sporadically throughout the book, but I found it important enough to sum up in on its own as it's essentially the process we need to find and continue healing in this experience. There are so many misconceptions about past lives, I will share what I have channeled and seen in my connections. You can have more than one life at a time and you are not your past lives! What does this mean? Every soul has a higher-self. Higher-self stays in soul form in the soul realm and is much like your parent soul. This is who we truly are, and this is our true essence, in whole. This essence encompasses all our consecutive lives, like a master puppeteer. There is no time in the soul dimension. Time is a human illusion. We create a system of time because our body is deteriorating and because our physical brain processes information in linear form, much like a computer. But none of that is necessary on soul dimension, therefore souls are not susceptible to the same restrictions we are. Our higher-selves are always looking to evolve ourselves so that we may reach nirvana, enlightenment, or oneness. Master and merge.

With this goal in mind, higher-self then takes fragments of itself and says, "In this life I will work on anger. In this life I will work through love. In this life I will work through...etc." In this way, all of your lives are fragments of higher-self. In this visual, our parallel lives are more like sibling souls all connected to the same parent soul or higher-self.

You can meet another fragment of your higher-self here on earth. You can come face-to-face. You can cross. But we don't usually write it that way so it's not common at all. Our twin flames are not fragments of our higher-self. Regarding twin flames, our higher-selves are vibrationally in-tune and interconnected. A team. This brings me to my next point, if a parent has 600 kids, regardless of parents being the same - each kid will be different. Just as siblings are different, our fragments of self are different and have personalities all their own. You may be more like one life then another, but essentially in every life you live you are a different fragment of higher-self. The only circumstance where this would not apply is if a soul "failed" their mission. This "failure" can look like suicide, accidental or unplanned death, or sometimes just lack of will power. Sometimes a failure is as simple as not accomplishing your charted goals. In this rare case, the soul usually gets thrown back into the same kind of life, usually with the same people, with the same soul fragment and the same obstructions. This is what we call **ancestral karma**. Many times, these lives can take generations to overcome and are the hardest cycles to break because we've lived them so many times. Even after we break the cycles, we may come back in to help the rest of the soul family follow through.

An example of this process might look like this: a gifted soul becomes overwhelmed by their gifts. They continue to block the emotional body. The emotional body will continue to obstruct and sicken the individual until their physical body is simply too heavy and burdened for healing in this life. In this case the body may stay stagnant, repeating the same day, energy, choices. Never looking for change but only survival. They may even take up drugs or inhibitors to mentally remove themselves from the process feeling a deep sense of failure they have embedded into their energy. Eventually this body will die, many times by suicide, overdose, or accident and then wake up on soul dimension or what people call "the other side". It is simply a world of energy, like all dimensions worlds and realms are places with different energetic densities. The soul dimension over laps our own, so our deceased loved ones are always close to us. When we read and connect to souls on soul dimension, we are pulling them through the veil, or the energy that separates our dimensions, so that we can communicate with them. Please note that every single experience is completely unique to the person, I am simply giving an example of a theme I have come across. After the soul awakens on soul side, the soul will likely throw itself back into the same family, because the connections were already planned and thought out, and try again. The issue is that many times they come in with their past life trauma already programmed right at birth. In this situation you are healing multiple lives at once – that is IF that soul can get strong and courageous enough to be the leader of change this time around. In this kind of situation, it can help to remove the "weight" by energetically cutting the past lives so that the person may only have to work to one life of baggage as opposed to multiple. But many times, healing and removal simply isn't allowed by our higher-selves because the lesson is one that needs to be physically worked through.

Why do past lives leak into our current existence? They leak for many reasons. Some past lives leak into our existence because of unfinished business or lessons. Some because of deep emotional triggers. Other past lives may linger because they need healing, some because they have a lesson to teach. Some just by accident. If we suffered deep trauma in a past life, especially before death, that trauma may haunt us in our current experience as fears, phobias, obstructions. For example, if we saw our loved one burned alive, we may carry a phobia of love and fire not understanding why. If we experienced a place crash, we may carry a phobia of plane crashes. Sometimes these traumatic deaths leave a haunting in the area they occurred. If a fragment of a soul is still haunting a place of death, then it will keep calling you for healing. Stuck souls or hauntings don't have very many resources for help because they are essentially stuck between dimensions, but you are one of them. In this case, releasing them from the trauma and haunting will allow you healing in your current existence.

Some past lives are inappropriately attached simply because we never healed from them to begin with. Some lives experience such intense trauma that it will damage, tear, rip our higher-self. In a situation like this, it may linger until you physically go in and repair the damage and heal the life energetically. These deep soul leaks will drain your energy and stunt healing in all lives. The reason why we cannot heal these at the energetic level is because they were created in the physical level and have physical traits to that damage. Many times, the body that experienced that trauma is also still suffering reliving the pain daily. In this way, it is necessary to heal the suffering life and the soul tear to find healing in this situation.

Other past lives may linger because they need healing. In this case they call upon us simply because they need help. They will express themselves with reoccurring patterns and behaviors until we understand and heal the patterns which assists the past life and current life at the same time.

If you are currently reliving an issue you have already learned, you may accidently trigger a past life where you already lived and suffered through the same lesson. This comes through as a reminder that you've already learned this, like a memory trying to help you remember the lesson, so you can make better decisions in this life.

Some lives can and will become triggered by accident. A good example of this is the twin flame versus soul-mate lives I explained earlier in the book. Your past life was triggered by coming into contact with a soul from your past life. It wasn't meant to be a trigger, it has no use in this life, it simply needs to be understood and released, like an energetic bond it can be cut.

It's important to note the information you gathered in past life journeying is always for growth and healing. Growth and evolution is our focus. Not who we were or what we did. Getting obsessed or stuck in our past life experiences can and will take our energy from this life and cause a vortex that will keep pulling energy from this life to our past lives, making us weaker on this plane. That's not something I wish upon myself or anyone else. We have all had dark lives because we have all had dark energies we had to work through. This doesn't make us dark. On the contrary, because we have had dark lives, we have worked through we now understand that darkness, what caused our and how to avoid the same reaction or fate. Keep that in mind. Many people create this vortex when they find they have a famous past life, for this reason I don't give names.

We can have past or future lives guide us in this life. If we have mastered a gift or lesson in another life, that past life may come through to assist us in developing that lesson or gift in this life. For example, I have a shaman guide, because I was a shaman. I have a witch guide, because I was a witch, I have an oracle guide, because I was an oracle. I have a gypsy guide, because I was a gypsy. I have a British psychic guide, because I was a psychic. Their lessons and assistance come forward to direct me in being the best version of myself in this current life. An accumulation of guides and gifts that I have separately worked though on other lives. I was also a mother of 3 in pastel suburbia, she doesn't come through as a gift guide because I didn't use my gifts in that life – even though I had them.

Lastly, all this information is useless if you refuse to retrain your physical body to respond differently to your environment. Soul and body are still very detached for most people. Meaning that we can heal the soul all day and night, but if you don't physically behave and respond differently you will pull in the same obstructions we have already removed. Example, someone who grew up with abuse might flinch or startle when someone raises their hand or voice even though they haven't been abused for 25 years. This is a response to abuse and if you wish to fully heal from abuse you must also heal your physical response to your environment. Our physical response is a reminder that there is still lingering pain that needs healing. If you truly want healing, remember to re-train the body and physically release what we retrieve and discover in these reports. Free will is our strongest gift or burden because your physical body can always reject soul healing through free will. You need to will and accept healing by continuing to retrain the physical body you move forward in your own healing process.

Without understanding soul development and past lives we are very disconnected from the soul evolution process. Being disconnected means we are simply letting this happen to us instead of being the divine creators of our reality. By understanding the process and the layers that make us the beautiful energetic beings that we are, we may begin to take charge of our own experience and truly shift the progression of souls on earth. I hope that you will use this information for your own self development and evolution, as did I.

Growing Pains

"Since the day I carried you in my womb, I wanted to protect you and nurture you. Someday my child you will wake up to the reality of a violent world. All of a sudden you will see and feel and hurt for all the pain humans cause each other. You will see the never necessary violence, hatred, judgment, and you will shed a tear. You may even wonder why I would bring you into such a violent world.

So my child, until this day... I will nurture you. Teach you love. Teach you empathy. Teach you kindness. And hold you tight. Because you see, what the world needs is more people like us. The world needs those who see and feel and jump into action to find solutions. Whether it be standing bold at a podium, running for office, marching with a group, or simply holding the hand of a friend in solidarity and support for their plea. The world needs more healing. More love. More kindness.

One day at a time. One act at a time. We will accomplish our mission. Remember that my child. You are not a victim, you are a necessary force of good, a guiding light."

-Jessenia Nozzolillo

Terms and their definitions

SOCIAL MEDIA LINKS AND BOOKING WEBSITE

Facebook: New England Psychic Medium
Website: https://www.NewEnglandPsychicMedium.com
Instagram: @New_England_psychic_medium

Printed in the United States
By Bookmasters